NUOVE MUSICHE E NUOVA MANIERA DI SCRIVERLE
(1614)

Recent Researches in the Music of the Baroque Era is one of four quarterly series (Middle Ages and Early Renaissance; Renaissance; Baroque Era; Classical Era) which make public the early music that is being brought to light in the course of current musicological research.

Each volume is devoted to works by a single composer or in a single genre of composition, chosen because of their potential interest to scholars and performers, and prepared for publication according to the standards that govern the making of all reliable historical editions.

Subscribers to this series, as well as patrons of subscribing institutions, are invited to apply for information about the "Copyright-Sharing Policy" of A-R Editions, Inc., under which the contents of this volume may be reproduced free of charge for performance use.

Correspondence should be addressed:

A-R Editions, Inc.
315 West Gorham Street
Madison, Wisconsin 53703

RECENT RESEARCHES IN THE MUSIC OF THE BAROQUE ERA • VOLUME XXVIII

Giulio Caccini

NUOVE MUSICHE E NUOVA MANIERA DI SCRIVERLE (1614)

Edited by H. Wiley Hitchcock

A-R EDITIONS, INC. • MADISON

Copyright © 1978, A-R Editions, Inc.

ISSN 0484-0828

ISBN 0-89579-105-6

Library of Congress Cataloging in Publication Data:

Caccini, Giulio, d. 1618?
  ₁Nuove musiche e nuova maniera di scriverle₁
  Nuove musiche e nuova maniera di scriverle : (1614).

  (Recent researches in the music of the baroque era ;
v. 28 ISSN 0484-0828)
  For Voice and continuo; figured bass realized for
keyboard instrument.
  1. Songs, Italian. I. Title. II. Series.
M2R238 vol. 28 ₁M1620₁ 780'.903'2s 78-15057
ISBN 0-89579-105-6   ₁784'.3061₁

Contents

Introduction

The present volume may be considered a companion to the edition of Giulio Caccini's *Le nuove musiche* of 1602 published as Volume IX of Recent Researches in the Music of the Baroque Era (Madison: A-R Editions, Inc., 1970). That publication included in its introduction a sketch of what we know—or knew at the time—about Caccini's life and works. Later research has amended some details and brought a few more to light.

The Composer

Usually called Giulio Romano in contemporary accounts, Caccini was indeed born in Rome, and his first teacher there was Giovanni Animuccia—at least, so says his longtime acquaintance Antonio Brunelli in a recently discovered volume of music by Brunelli dedicated to "Il Signor Giulio Caccini di Roma."[1] Brunelli's dedication corroborates Caccini's claim (in the preface to *Le nuove musiche*) that he had been in the service of the Medici since 1565, when he would have been about twenty years old: Caccini was brought to Florence in the mid-1560s at the behest of Cosimo I de' Medici, Grand Duke of Tuscany, who may first have heard him sing during a ducal visit to Rome in 1560. In Florence, Cosimo supported Caccini in further musical studies with Scipione delle Palle, to whom Brunelli refers as "the foremost singer" of the century. Caccini was to remain at the Medici court (except for a winter-long sojourn in Paris in 1604/5, at the court of Henri IV and his queen, the former Maria de' Medici) until his death in 1618, when he was buried in one of Florence's most prestigious churches, SS. Annunziata. Thus, *Nuove musiche e nuova maniera di scriverle* was a work of the composer's old age; in fact, published in 1614, when Caccini would have been almost seventy, this second (and last) of his songbooks was to be his *opus ultimum*.[2]

This "other" *Nuove musiche*—to which we shall refer as "*Nuove musiche* (1614)," to distinguish it from *Le nuove musiche* of 1602—is exceedingly rare and little-known: only two copies seem presently to exist (one, on which the present edition is based, at the Biblioteca Nazionale Centrale, Florence; the other at the British Library, London), and no second or later editions were printed. The present volume comprises the first modern scholarly/practical version of the songbook.[3]

The Plan of Nuove musiche (1614)

The plan of *Nuove musiche* (1614) resembles that of its predecessor. Appearing first in the volume is a dedication to a noble patron, in this instance Caccini's first supporter, Piero Falconieri, a member of the Roman branch of an old Florentine family. There follows a preface by the composer, briefer than the famous "discourse" on song and singing of *Le nuove musiche* but not without interest. The main body of the book contains two series of songs for solo voice and basso continuo; the first is a series on monostrophic, madrigalesque poems, the second a series of strophic songs on canzonet-like poems with from two to eleven strophes each. Between the two song series is a kind of centerpiece (as, in *Le nuove musiche*, music from the pastorale *Il rapimento di Cefalo* provides a centerpiece); this is made up of "Torna, deh torna" [17], a song in the form of strophic variations based on the *Romanesca* air-and-bass, and two "special airs for tenor, who explores the bass range" [18-19] (as Caccini describes them on the title page). The latter two songs cover a very wide vocal range of more than two and one-half octaves, from g' down to C, and both songs are multipartite: the first [18a-d] is based on the poetic divisions (two quatrains, two tercets) of a sonnet; the second [19a-b] has two interrelated *partes*, each of which is a two-stanza strophic air. (Similarly, among the first series of madrigalesque songs, a Petrarch sonnet is divided by Caccini according to the quatrains and tercets to fashion the multipartite group [16a-d].)

In sum, *Nuove musiche* (1614) contains twenty-nine songs, three of them—[16], [18], and [19]—in several *partes*. Thus, it is a bulkier collection than *Le nuove musiche* (which contains twenty-two songs plus the excerpt from *Il rapimento di Cefalo*) and is in fact larger than any monodic songbook that had been published before.

The poets of the collection are largely the same ones to whose works Caccini had turned for *Le nuove musiche*, and the frequency of appearance of poems by them is similar: verses by Ottavio Rinuccini appear most often; they are followed in frequency by poems of Gabriello Chiabrera and, next, Giovanni Battista Guarini. Poems by Petrarch and Giovanni della Casa, whose sonnets are the basis for the two quadripartite songs, [16] and [18], had not appeared in *Le nuove musiche*. Also new to the 1614 book are Torquato Tasso and Maria Menadori, each represented by one poem. The eleven "anonymous" poems—i.e., those whose authors have not yet been uncovered by the research which led to the identification of the other poems' authors (for none of the poets is cited in Caccini's volume)—show the influence, not apparent in *Le nuove musiche*, of the exuberant (not to say extravagant) metaphors, similes, and involutions of Giambattista Marino and his followers.

The Edition

This is not the place for an extended analysis of the music of *Nuove musiche* (1614). However, since any approach to editing the songbook must hinge on an interpretation of Caccini's statement (in his title) that the volume embodies not only "new pieces of music" but a "new way of writing them out," the music must be considered in light of that statement and of the composer's prefatory remarks.

The basic musical style of *Nuove musiche* (1614) differs but little from that of *Le nuove musiche*, except in details which suggest that Caccini's ears had not been entirely closed, during the dozen years that separated the two collections, to the work of progressive younger Italian composers. Nor does the notation of *Nuove musiche* (1614) differ from that of the first book: the "new way" of writing out his music to which his title refers is as much the basis of the 1602 publication as of that of 1614, as Caccini himself intimates in the preface to the latter, when he says, ". . . I have decided to publish now some other works of mine . . . written in the same manner, suitable for singing, since I have indicated in the voice part tremolos, trills, and other new effects not often seen in print, with diminutions that are most appropriate for the voice." Caccini is more specific about the "nuova maniera di scriverle" when he speaks about "my style of solo singing, which I write out exactly as it is sung," and he even proclaims on the title page that in *Nuove musiche* (1614) "it is shown that with this new way . . . all the delicacies of this art can be learned without having to hear the composer sing." (In other words, the singing style can be learned just by reading what is written on the page.) In sum, in both songbooks the "new way" of writing out the music consists of including *in print* various ornaments and decorative *passaggi* normally, in Caccini's time, improvised by singers.[4]

This being true, the same editorial approach may be made to *Nuove musiche* (1614) as to *Le nuove musiche*, and this has been done in the present volume, with the few exceptions noted below. For the general editorial principles, the reader is referred to the comments on "The Present Edition" in RECENT RESEARCHES IN THE MUSIC OF THE BAROQUE ERA, IX, pp. 11-13. It is important to remember that, as clarified in his preface of 1602, there are a few kinds of ornaments which Caccini does *not* write out fully in musical notation. He occasionally indicates, by means of abbreviated verbal cues, where a singer may add such ornaments; however, according to our reading of the 1602 preface, still others may be added judiciously (as they have been, editorially, in the music that follows). The ornaments involved, and the editorial abbreviations for them, are:

[tr] = tremolo (not trill, although Caccini called it *trillo*): a rapid reiteration of the same pitch, perhaps accelerating if found on a long note, but if so not in measured rhythm.

[gr] = trill (Caccini's *gruppo*): a similarly rapid (and perhaps accelerating) unmeasured alternation of the written pitch with one a second above, ending if possible with a turn.

[<>] = Caccini's *crescere e scemare della voce*: a crescendo-and-decrescendo, applied to single notes of long duration.

[escl] = Caccini's *esclamazione*: essentially a decrescendo-and-crescendo on a single pitch, most commonly found at the beginning of a phrase.

Editorial alterations of or additions to the 1614 print are made directly in the musical text wherever possible, and are enclosed in square brackets. Editorial changes which cannot thus be made clearly in the musical text are explained in the Textual Commentary.

Three differences in editorial procedure from that used for the publication of *Le nuove musiche* should be explained here.

First, although in his basso continuo figuration Caccini always uses the sign ♯ to indicate a major third (i.e., a major triad) over the bass note, and the sign ♭ to indicate a minor third (i.e., a minor triad), wherever the modern ♮ sign, in a given context, makes the desired realization clearer to present-day accompanists, the ♮ has been substituted for Caccini's figure. (Thus, ♮ over a G indicates a G-major triad, ♮ over a D, a D-minor triad.)

Second, when Caccini wishes one or more changes of harmony over a single bass note, he divides the note into the appropriate segments and ties them (e.g., ♩͟ ♩). This notation has the virtue of indicating the precise duration of each note or chord of the realization. However, in an edition such as this one, which offers a possible realization of the continuo part, preserving the tied-note notation seems pedantic, and such notes have been reduced to single full values. (Caccini is explicit, in the preface to *Le nuove musiche*, that such tied notes in the continuo part are not to be restruck, so the altered notation does no violence to his intention.)

Third, the suggestions for rhythmic resolutions of poetic elisions that were included in the edition of *Le nuove musiche* were, on reflection, an editorial error. These suggestions tend to congeal, even to freeze, the rhythmic life of the voice part—to rob it of some of its desirable *sprezzatura*—and they do not appear in the present edition.

Acknowledgments

This edition was prepared in Florence, from a base at Villa I Tatti (the Harvard University Center for Italian Renaissance Studies). To the former director of I Tatti, Professor Myron P. Gilmore, and its present director, Professor Craig Hugh Smyth, I am most grateful for hospitality and encouragement. My work was greatly facilitated by the music collection, established by Elizabeth and Gordon Morrill, in I Tatti's Biblioteca Berenson, and by the accommodating staff in the manuscript room of the Biblioteca Nazionale Centrale, Firenze. To the latter library, appreciation is also due for permission to reproduce several pages of *Nuove musiche* (1614). Anita Plotinsky, as a seminar student, first pointed out to me the authorship of one of the "special airs" [18]. Anna Terni and, especially, Fiorella Gioffredi Superbi (both of Villa I Tatti) were of great help in untangling the knots of both thought and typography in the poems of the songbook. As al-

ways, my wife Janet provided good-humored, incisive, and constructive criticism. Finally, for unselfishly assisting me over many years with problems of Italian monody in general and *Nuove musiche* (1614) in particular, Nigel Fortune, of the University of Birmingham, has my warmest gratitude; to him I dedicate my share of the present publication.

H. Wiley Hitchcock
(Brooklyn College of the
City University of New York)

Florence, 1976

Notes

[1]See H. W. Hitchcock, "A New Biographical Source for Caccini," *Journal of the American Musicological Society* XXVI (1973): 145-7.

[2]For a general discussion of *Nuove musiche e nuova maniera di scriverle*, see Hitchcock, "Caccini's 'Other' *Nuove musiche*," *Journal of the American Musicological Society* XXVII (1974): 438-60. A third book of songs, *Fuggilotio musicale* (Venice, 1613), attributed on its title page to "D. Giulio Romano" and cited as by Caccini (although with many reservations) in the edition of *Le nuove musiche*, has been shown to be the work of another composer. See Hitchcock, "Depriving Caccini of a Musical Pastime," *Journal of the American Musicological Society* XXV (1972): 58-78.

[3]We are aware, in making this statement, of the volume titled *Giulio Caccini: Le* [sic] *Nuove musiche, Firenze 1614* (Florence: Cen-

tro Studi Rinascimento Musicale, 1975), eds. N. Anfuso and A. Gianuario, which was published as the present edition was nearing completion. This "edition" of *Nuove musiche* (1614), despite a luxurious format, is error-ridden, follows uniquely idiosyncratic editorial procedures, and is unperformable by all but clairvoyant musicians; it also includes photofacsimiles of the entire 1614 print, which are, however, poorly photographed and so reduced in size as to be illegible.

[4]The arguments for this interpretation are presented in Hitchcock, "Vocal Ornamentation in Caccini's *Nuove musiche*," *Musical Quarterly* LVI (1970): 389-404, and in the articles cited in note 2 above.

Textual Commentary

This commentary includes the following sorts of information for each song in the unique 1614 edition of *Nuove musiche e nuova maniera di scriverle* (numbered in order of appearance in the source): the poetic text, with an English version (not a literal, let alone a singable, translation, but a close paraphrase); identification of the author if known, and brief analytic comments on the poem; citation of manuscript versions and later editions; location in the 1614 print; and description of the *original* musical text for any passages altered editorially without indication. Wherever necessary alterations could be made simply and clearly in the edition itself, they have been enclosed there in square brackets; these bracketed alterations are not cited here.

[1] A quei sospir ardenti

Text

A quei sospir ardenti
Che fingesti esalar per troppo ardore,
A quei dolci lamenti
Misti d'amare lagrime d'amore
Credulo amant' a pers' il seno e il core.
Nè d'amoroso strale
Schivai colpo mortale.
Al fin arso e ferito
E deluso e schernito
E veggio e sento
Ch'i pianti e i sospir miei son acqua e vento.

[To those ardent sighs that you pretended to breathe out of uncontrollable ardor, to those sweet laments mingled with bitter tears of love, this credulous lover has lost his heart. Nor have I avoided the mortal wound of Cupid's arrow. Finally—burned, wounded, deluded, mocked—I realize that my own tears and sighs are naught but water and wind.]

The author is probably Ottavio Rinuccini: a version concording well with that of *Nuove musiche* (1614) is in Florence, Biblioteca Nazionale, Codex Palatino 249 (attributed to Rinuccini), fol. 68. The poem is an eleven-line madrigal in *settenario* and *endecasillabo* verses, with the rhyme and meter scheme $a^7 b^{11} a^7 b^{11} b^{11} c^7 c^7 d^7 d^7 e^7 e^{11}$.

Music

Ms. versions:

(None located)

Nuove musiche (1614), pp. 1-3:

m. 4, voice: The second and third E's are natural.

m. 10, voice: The last two E's are natural. The rhythm of beats 3 and 4 is ♫♫♫ ♫♫♫ (unbeamed).

m. 16, voice: The second F is natural.

m. 21, voice: The second and third F's are natural.

m. 23, voice: The last three F's are natural.

mm. 25-26, voice: All the E's are natural.

m. 36, voice: The second E is natural.

m. 47, voice: The second E is natural.

m. 50, voice: The second E is natural.

m. 54, voice: The second E is natural.

m. 55, voice: The second and third F's are natural.

m. 56, voice: The last three F's are natural.

[2] Alme luci beate

Text

Alme luci beate
Che dolcemente ardeste
E dolce distruggeste
L'incenerito core,
Chi di bei lampi or farà lieto Amore?
Io vi lasso mie scorte,
Io mi parto bei numi,
Io vò lungi miei numi,
E non ho spem' ohimè che mi conforte.
Alme luci beate,
Se per si lunga etate
Amando e rimirando
Voi foste il mio gioire,
Or per si lunga etate
Amando e rimembrando
Sarete il mio martire.

[Divine lights that sweetly burned and consumed my ashen heart, whom will Love now delight with your lovely flashes? I leave you, my beacons; I depart for distant parts, my divine ones; and I have no more hope to comfort me. Divine lights, if for so long, loving and gazing, you were my delight, now, for just as long, loving and remembering, you will be my martyrdom.]

The author is unidentified. The poem is a sixteen-line madrigal in *settenario* and *endecasillabo* verses, with the rhyme and meter scheme $a^7 b^7 b^7 c^7 c^{11} d^7 e^7 e^7 d^{11} a^7 a^7 f^7 g^7 a^7 f^7 g^7$.

Music

Ms. versions:

(None located)

Nuove musiche (1614), pp. 3-5:

m. 22, voice: The second C is natural.

m. 44, bass: The G is figured sharp (i.e., B natural).

m. 46, voice: The sharp follows the first F.

m. 51, voice: The rhythm of the first two notes is dotted eighth, sixteenth.

m. 53, bass: The sharp figure follows the first D (but is not quite aligned with the second; possibly only the second of the two chords is to be major).

[3] Se in questo scolorito languido volto

Text

Se in questo scolorito
Languido volto amar non puoi bellezza,
Ama fede, am' amore, ama fermezza
In questo cor ferito.
Non è d'amor più degno
D'una fiorita guancia un cor fedele?
Ma tu pur sempre l'amorose vele
Spieghi all'usato segno.
Ahi! non vedrò mai il di, ch'a me le giri,
Mosse dal vento di tanti sospiri?

[If in this pale, drooping countenance you can find no beauty to love, love in this wounded heart its fidelity, love, constancy. Is not a faithful heart more worthy of love than a blooming cheek? But, as always, you unfurl your amorous sails to the old sign. Oh! shall I never see the day that will bring them back to me, blown by the wind of so many sighs?]

The author is either Gabriello Chiabrera or Ottavio Rinuccini. With three minor variants , the poem (with the title "Amante brutto") is given in Chiabrera, *Canzonette, rime varie, dialoghi*, ed. Luigi Negri (Turin: U.T.E.T., 1952), p. 63. In a version with a first line closer than Chiabrera's to that of *Nuove musiche* (1614), it appears in *Poesie del Sᵣ Ottavio Rinuccini* (Florence: I Giunti, 1622), p. 59; the same version appears in Florence, Biblioteca Nazionale, Codex Palatino 249 (attributed to Rinuccini), fol. 119. The poem is a ten-line madrigal, with the rhyme and meter scheme a^7 b^{11} b^{11} a^7 c^7 d^{11} d^{11} c^7 e^{11} e^{11}.

Music

Ms. versions:

(None located)

Nuove musiche (1614), pp. 5-6:

m. 13, voice: The second and third F's are natural.

m. 27, voice: The G is as given here; but note that in the repetition of the phrase (m. 43) it is sharp.

m. 53, voice: All the F's are natural.

[4] S'io vivo, anima mia

Text

S'io vivo, anima mia, vivo per voi
E se languisco e moro
Mi fate voi morire,

Mi fate voi languire,
E languendo e morendo ancor v'adoro.
Ma se di voi si bell' e si vitale
Vien' effetto mortale,
Ah! cruda è vostra colpa, o pur mia sorte
Che siate vita e volet' esser morte.

[If I live, my beloved, I live for you; and if I languish and die, it is you who make me do so; and yet, languishing and dying, I still adore you. But if from you, so lovely and lively, comes the deadly end, ah! harsh is your stroke (or rather my lot), for you who are life wish to be death.]

The author is unidentified. The poem is a nine-line madrigal in *settenario* and *endecasillabo* verses, with the rhyme and meter scheme a^{11} b^7 c^7 c^7 b^{11} d^{11} d^7 e^{11} e^{11}.

Music

Ms. versions:

(None located)

Nuove musiche (1614), pp. 6-7:

m. 10, voice: The last three F's are natural.

m. 12, voice: Only the second C is sharp.

m. 17, voice: The first F is natural.

m. 18, voice: The rhythm of the last half of the measure is ♫♫♫ (unbeamed).

m. 19, voice: The last F is natural.

m. 30, bass: The third note is C.

mm. 35-36, voice: Text underlay is "ta-le"; corrected by analogy with mm. 34, 51-52, and 53-57.

[5] Se ridete gioiose

Text

Se ridete gioiose,
Dolci labbra amorose,
Non sa mostrarne Amore
Pregio d'amor maggiore
In alcun nobil viso,
Che il vostro bel sorriso;
E pur ne mostra Amore
Pregio d'amor maggiore
Nel vostro nobil viso,
Col lampeggiar d'un riso,
Se ridono gioiosi
Gli occhi vostri amorosi.

[If, sweet loving lips, you laugh joyously, Love knows not how to decorate a noble face with anything more worthy of love than your splendid smile. But Love does indeed offer something even more loveworthy when, with the flash of a laugh, your loving eyes laugh joyously.]

The author is Gabriello Chiabrera; see, under the title "Loda gli occhi," *I lirici del seicento e dell'Arcadia*, ed. Carlo Calcaterra (Milan, Rome: Rizzoli, 1936), p.

295. The poem is a twelve-line madrigal wholly in *settenario* verses, with the rhyme scheme *a a b b c c b b c c d d*.

MUSIC

Editions:

  1. Antonio Brunelli, *Scherzi, arie, canzonette, e madrigali* . . . (Venice: G. Vincenti, 1614), p. 28.

Nuove musiche (1614), pp. 8-9.

[6] Ohimè, begli occhi

TEXT

Ohimè, begli occhi, e quando
Di mai più rivedervi havrò speranza
Se pria ch'io giung' al tempo del partire
Già mi sento morire?
Spenderò lagrimando
Questo poco di vita che m'avanza,
E 'n dura lontananza
Pur sempr' invan bramando
I vostri dolci rai,
Tanto vi piangerò quant'io v'amai.

[Alas, beauteous eyes, when shall I ever hope to see you again if, even before departing, I already feel myself dying? I shall spend the little life left to me weeping and, far away from you, still vainly longing for your sweet glances, I shall weep for you as much as I have loved you.]

The author is unidentified. An unattributed version concording perfectly with that of *Nuove musiche* (1614) is in Florence, Biblioteca Nazionale, Codex Palatino 251, p. 257 (No. 158). The poem is a ten-line madrigal in *settenario* and *endecasillabo* verses, with the rhyme and meter scheme $a^7\ b^{11}\ c^{11}\ c^7\ d^7\ b^{11}\ b^7\ d^7\ e^7\ e^{11}$.

MUSIC

Ms. versions:

  1. Florence, Cons., Ms. Barbera, fol. [76].

Nuove musiche (1614), pp. 10-11:

  m. 18, voice: The first C is a sixteenth-note.
  m. 42, voice: The G is sharped.
  m. 50, voice: The last three C's are natural.

[7] Dite o del foco mio

TEXT

Dite o del foco mio
Bellissima cagion, luci spietate,
E pur volete ch'io,
Senza sperar già mai,
Incontro al folgorar de' vostri rai,
Schermo alcun di pietate,
Amando e desiando mi consumi.

Ah! dolcissimi lumi,
Non vedete negli occhi aperto il core
Che cener fatt' ancor si strugg'e more?

[Tell me, o glorious source of my ardor—pitiless eyes, do you really want me to have no hope of any shield of pity against the fire of your rays, but rather, loving and desiring, to be consumed? Ah, sweetest lights! do you not see my cindered heart melting, dying?]

The author is unidentified. An unattributed version concording perfectly with that of *Nuove musiche* (1614) is in Florence, Biblioteca Nazionale, Codex Palatino 251, p. 90 (No. LI). The poem is a ten-line madrigal in *settenario* and *endecasillabo* verses, with the rhyme and meter scheme $a^7\ b^{11}\ a^7\ c^7\ c^{11}\ b^7\ d^{11}\ d^7\ e^{11}\ e^{11}$.

MUSIC

Ms. versions:

  (None located)

Nuove musiche (1614), pp. 11-12:

  m. 18, voice: The second F is natural.
  m. 31, voice: The last three C's are natural.
  m. 29a, voice: The last three C's are natural.

[8] O' dolce fonte del mio pianto

TEXT

O' dolce fonte del mio pianto amaro
È pur ver ch'io qui miri
Bagnar que' duo begli occhi à miei sospiri;
È ver che rispondiat' a miei lamenti
Con interrotti accenti?
O' di per me beato,
O' fortunato e caro,
Spezzato è 'l sasso ch'indurò quell'alma,
E la tempesta mia rivolta in calma.

[O sweet fount of my bitter grief, is it really true that now I see those two lovely eyes bathed in my sighs? Is it true that you respond to my laments with choked speech? O blessed, lucky day! Broken is the stone-hardened soul; calmed is my tempest.]

The author is unidentified. An unattributed version concording well with that of *Nuove musiche* (1614) is in Florence, Biblioteca Nazionale, Codex Palatino 251, p. 91 (No. LII), where it follows "Dite o del foco mio," as it does here. The poem is a nine-line madrigal in *settenario* and *endecasillabo* verses, with the rhyme and meter scheme $a^{11}\ b^7\ b^{11}\ c^{11}\ c^7\ d^7\ e^7\ f^{11}\ f^{11}$.

MUSIC

Ms. versions:

  1. Modena, Bibl. Estense, Ms. Mus.F.1526, fol. 12ᵛ-13ᵛ.

Nuove musiche (1614), pp. 13-14.

[9] Ch'io non t'ami cor mio

TEXT

Ch'io non t'ami cor mio
Ch'io non sia la tua vit' e tu la mia,
Che per nuovo desio
E per nuova bellezza io t'abbandoni,
Prima che questo sia
Morte non mi perdoni.
Ma se tu sei quel cor onde la vita
M'è si dolc'e gradita,
Fonte d'ogni mio ben, d'ogni desire,
Come posso lassarti e non morire?

[Should I not love you, my heart's desire; should I not be your life and you mine; should I abandon you for a new beauty—before any of that, death should not spare me. But since yours is the heart whence springs my sweet life, fount of my well-being and of every desire, how can I leave you and not die?]

The author is Giovanni Battista Guarini; see G. B. Guarini, *Rime* (Venice: Ciotti, 1621), p. 296 (No. LXXXIV), where the poem appears with the title "Amor costante." The poem is a ten-line madrigal in *settenario* and *endecasillabo* verses, with the rhyme and meter scheme $a^7 b^{11} a^7 c^{11} b^7 c^7 d^{11} d^7 e^{11} e^{11}$.

MUSIC

Ms. versions:

1. Florence, Bibl. Naz., Ms. Magl. XIX.66, fol. [40]-[40ᵛ].
2. Brussels, Bibl. du Cons., Ms. 704, p. 30.

Nuove musiche (1614), pp. 14-15:

m. 21, bass: The last figure is ♯6; corrected by analogy with m. 31.

[10] Hor che lungi da voi

TEXT

Hor che lungi da voi
Muovo, bei lumi, ov'ha riposto Amore
Il più caro e 'l più bel de' lumi suoi
Chi da conforto al core?
Ahi che languire, ahi che perir il sento!
Lasso! ben gran tormento
È sostener, amand' orgogli ed ire;
Ma chi disse partir, disse morire.

[Now that I wander far from you, lights of my life, wherein Love has lodged his most beauteous glances, who can comfort me? Ah, how I feel me languishing, dying! Alas, though it is great torment to be near, loving pride and anger, to say farewell is to speak of death.]

The author is Gabriello Chiabrera. Caccini uses only the first of three stanzas; see Chiabrera, *Canzonette, rime varie, dialoghi,* ed. Luigi Negri (Turin: U.T.E.T., 1952), pp. 97-8, which gives the complete poem under the title "Che essendo lontano dalla sua donna, soffre gran pene, ma che desidera e spera di rivederla." The single, madrigalesque stanza (like each of the others of the complete poem) is in *settenario* and *endecasillabo* verses, with the rhyme and meter scheme $a^7 b^{11} a^{11} b^7 c^{11} c^7 d^{11} d^{11}$.

MUSIC

Ms. versions:

1. Tenbury, St. Michael's College, Ms. 1018, fol. 43.

Nuove musiche (1614), pp. 15-16:

m. 29, voice: First note is an eighth-note.

[11] Pien d'amoroso affetto

TEXT

Pien d'amoroso affetto
Tirsi a Filli dicea:
Deh trafiggim'il petto
S'hai ch'io mora diletto.
Così dolce per lei languendo ardea.
Ella spario di rose
Il suo bel volto e poi così rispose:
Io di morte son vaga,
Ma da te la desio,
Dolcissimo cor mio;
Da si bel feritor dolc'è la piaga.

[Full of love, Thyrsis said to Phyllis: "Ah! stab this breast, if you would that I die." (Thus did he burn, languishing, for her.) She strewed with roses his handsome face and then replied: " 'Tis I who wish death, but caused by you, my sweetheart: sweet would be the wound from so fine a wounder."]

The author is unidentified. The poem is an eleven-line madrigal in *settenario* and *endecasillabo* verses, with the rhyme and meter scheme $a^7 b^7 a^7 a^7 b^{11} c^7 c^{11} d^7 e^7 e^7 d^{11}$.

MUSIC

Ms. versions:

(None located)

Nuove musiche (1614), pp. 17-18:

m. 28, voice: The last three F's are natural.

[12] Amor l'ali m'impenna

TEXT

Amor l'ali m'impenna,
Amor dolce, amor caro, amor felice,
Tal che non spero più ne più mi lice.
Passo monti e procelle,

Passo 'l ciel e le stelle.
Del piacer quest'è 'l regno:
Ah, mia fortuna non se l'abbia a sdegno!
Questo, questo m'accora,
Ch'altri cadeo del paradiso ancora.

[Love feathers my wings—sweet, dear, happy love—
so that I hope for no more, nor more may have. I
vault mountains, storms, heavens, the stars! This is
the height of pleasure! Ah, but let not fortune be angry (for I realize with sorrow that others have fallen
from paradise).]

The author is Torquato Tasso; see No. LXI of his
"Rime amorose extravaganti" in Tasso, *Poesie,* ed.
Francesco Flora (Milan, Rome: Rizzoli, 1934), p. 739.
The poem is a nine-line madrigal in *settenario* and *en-
decasillabo* verses, with the rhyme and meter scheme
$a^7 \ b^{11} \ b^{11} \ c^7 \ c^7 \ d^7 \ d^{11} \ e^7 \ e^{11}$.

MUSIC

Ms. versions:

1. Florence, Bibl. Naz., Ms. Magl. XIX.66, fol. [33^v]-
   [34^v].
2. Brussels, Bibl. du Cons., Ms. 704, p. 32.
3. Tenbury, St. Michael's College, Ms. 1018, fol.
   43.

Nuove musiche (1614), pp. 18-19:

m. 22, voice: The second quarter is D, corrected in
   light of the figuration 11 (implying a $\frac{6}{4}$ chord)
   and the Ms. versions, which give E here and
   at the point corresponding to m. 32.

[13] Se voi lagrime a pieno

TEXT

Se voi lagrime a pieno
Non mostrate il dolore
Ch'entro racchiude il seno,
A che versate fore?
Statevi dentro e soffocat' il core.

[If, ye tears, you do not reveal completely the grief
contained in my breast, why do you fall? Stay within
and smother my heart.]

The author is unidentified. The poem is a five-line
madrigal in *settenario* and *endecasillabo* verses, with the
rhyme and meter scheme $a^7 \ b^7 \ a^7 \ b^7 \ b^{11}$.

MUSIC

Ms. versions:

(None located)

Nuove musiche (1614), pp. 19-20:

m. 12, bass: The last figure is ♯6.
m. 37, voice: The second G is natural.

[14] Vaga su spin'ascosa

TEXT

Vaga su spin'ascosa
È rosa rugiadosa,
Ch'all'alba si diletta,
Mossa da fresc'auretta;
Ma più vaga la rosa
Sulla guancia amorosa,
Ch'oscura e discolora
Le guance dell'Aurora:
Addio, Ninfa de' fiori,
E Ninfa degli odori,
Primavera gentile,
Statti pur con aprile;
Che più vaga e più vera
Mirasi primavera
Su quella fresca rosa
Della guancia amorosa,
Ch'oscura e discolora
Le guance dell'Aurora.

[Pretty is the dewy rose on the hidden thorn; it de-
lights in the dawn and is shaken by the breeze. But
prettier still is the rose on an amorous cheek, which
puts to shame the rosiness of dawn. Farewell, flower-
nymph and nymph of aromas: gentle spring, remain
with April; admire yourself more in that fresh rose
of the amorous cheek, which puts to shame the rosiness of dawn.]

The author is Gabriello Chiabrera; see, under the
title "Loda le guance," *I lirici del seicento e dell'Arcadia,*
ed. Carlo Calcaterra (Milan, Rome: Rizzoli, 1936), p.
294. The poem is a canzonet in nine rhymed cou-
plets, entirely in *settenario* verses, with the rhyme
scheme *aa bb aa cc dd ee ff aa cc.*

MUSIC

Ms. versions:

1. Brussels, Bibl. du Cons., Ms. 704, pp. 161-2.

Nuove musiche (1614), pp. 25-6 (*recte* 21-2):

mm. 19-20, voice: The rhythm is ♩ ♩ ♪ ♪♪ ♩ ♪
   (etc.).
m. 28, voice: The second F is natural.
m. 29, voice: The last B is flat.
m. 31, voice: ♪♪♪ ♩ ♩ may have been
   intended. a-mo- ro- sa
m. 37a: The second ending is editorial.

[15] La bella man vi stringo

TEXT

La bella man vi stringo
E voi le ciglia per dolor stringete
E mi chiamate ingiusto, et inhumano,
Come tutto il gioire

Sia mio, vostro il martire;
E voi non v'accorgete
Che se questa è la mano
Che tien stretto il cor mio, giust'è'l dolore,
Perchè stringendo lei stringo il mio core.

[I squeeze your hand, and you knit your brows and call me unfair and inhuman, as if all joy were mine, martyrdom your lot. But you do not realize that if this is the hand that has captured my heart, your grief is right and proper, since by squeezing it I wring my heart.]

The author is Giovanni Battista Guarini; see, under the title "Mano stretta," *Rime del molto illustre Signor Cavaliere Battista Guarini . . .* (Venice: Ciotti, 1598), fol. 88. The poem is a nine-line madrigal in *settenario* and *endecasillabo* verses, with the rhyme and meter scheme $a^7 \ b^{11} \ c^{11} \ d^7 \ d^7 \ b^7 \ c^7 \ e^{11} \ e^{11}$.

Music

Ms. versions:

(None located)

Nuove musiche (1614), pp. 26-7 (*recte* 22-3):

m. 16, bass: Since the E-flats of the preceding "measure" (mm. 15-16 are a single measure in the source) are not explicitly altered here, Caccini may have intended this one as flat, too.

m. 32, bass: (See above note.)

[16a] Tutto 'l dì piango
[16b] In tristo umor
[16c] Lasso, che pur
[16d] Più l'altrui fallo

Text

Tutto 'l dì piango, e poi la notte, quando
Prendon riposo i miseri mortali,
Trovomi in pianto, e raddoppiarsi i mali;
Così spendo 'l mio tempo lagrimando.

In tristo umor vo li occhi consumando,
E 'l cor in doglia; e son fra li animali
L'ultimo, sì che li amorosi strali
Mi tengon ad ogni or di pace in bando.

Lasso, che pur da l'un a l'altro sole
E da l'un' ombra a l'altra, ò già 'l più corso
Di questa morte che si chiama vita.

Più l'altrui fallo che 'l mi' mal mi dole,
Ché pietà viva e 'l mio fido soccorso
Vedem' arder nel foco, e non m'aita.

[(a) I weep all the day; and then at night, when wretched mortals take rest, I find myself in tears, my ills redoubled: thus do I pass my time in tears. (b) In sad state I go, weeping my eyes out, my heart aching; and, dragging last after all other beings, I am kept continuously from peace by love's arrows. (c) Alas! from one sun to another, and from one dark to another, I have already almost run the course of this death called life. (d) Others' faults pain me more than my grief; O that Pity—alive, my faithful helper—should see me burning in flames and help me not!]

The author is Francesco Petrarca. Caccini sets this sonnet in four *partes*; see Petrarca, *Canzoniere*, ed. Gianfranco Contini (Turin: Einaudi, 1964), p. 278 (No. CCXVI): [16a] = lines 1-4, [16b] = 5-8, [16c] = 9-11, and [16d] = 12-14.

Music

Ms. versions:

(None located)

Editions:

1. ([16a] only; bass not realized, barring as in original): in Lorenzo Bianconi, "Caccini e il manierismo musicale," *Chigiana* XXV (1968): 35.

Nuove musiche (1614), pp. 27-30 (*recte* 23-6):

m. 35, voice: Caccini may have intended the F to be sharped.
m. 36, voice: The second F is natural.
m. 37, voice: The second F is natural.
m. 50, voice: The second F is natural.
m. 51, voice: The second F is natural.
m. 57, voice: The second F is natural.
m. 64, voice: The second F is natural.
m. 67, voice: The second half of the measure is ♫♫♪ (unbeamed).
m. 80, voice: The last three E's are natural.
m. 83, voice: The second F is natural.
m. 103, voice: The last beat is ♪ ♪♪♪.

[17] Torna, deh torna [Romanesca]

Text

Torna, deh torna pargoletto mio,
Torna, che senza te son senza core!
Dove t'ascondi, ohimè? che t'ho fatt' io,
Ch'io non ti veggio e non ti sento, Amore?
Corrimi in braccio omai, spargi d'oblio
Questo, che 'l cuor mi strugge, aspro dolore.
Senti de la mia voce il flebil suono
Tra' pianti e tra' sospir' chieder perdono.

[Return, my little one! Return, for without you I am without my heart! Where do you hide, alas? What have I done that I neither see nor hear you, love? Fly now to my arms; dissolve that bitter pain which consumes my heart. Hear the plaintive sound of my voice, begging forgiveness with tears and sighs.]

The author is Ottavio Rinuccini. The text is a portion of the speech of Venus (following the intermezzo in Part II) in Rinuccini's *Mascherata di ninfe di Senna* (1611; revised 1613), which is given complete in Angelo Solerti, *Gli albori del melodramma* (Milan, Palermo, Naples: R. Sandron, 1904; reprinted Hildesheim: G. Olms, 1969), II: 266-82; the present passage is found on p. 278. The poem is an *ottava rima* entirely in *endecasillabo* verses, with the conventional rhyme scheme *a b a b a b c c*.

MUSIC

Ms. versions:

(None located)

Nuove musiche (1614), pp. 30-2 (*recte* 26-8):

    m. 3, voice: The last half of the measure is ♫♪ (unbeamed).

    m. 12, voice: All three E's are natural. The rhythm for "che" is ꜇ ♪ ♫♫ (unbeamed).

    m. 18, voice: The second E is natural.

    m. 29, voice: The second E is natural.

    m. 45, voice: The second and third E's are natural. The last beat is notated as ♩. ♪ .

    m. 47, voice:

 (etc.)
(unbeamed).

    m. 52, voice: The second E is natural.

    m. 57, voice: The second E is natural.

    m. 64, voice: The second F is natural.

[18a] Io, che l'età solea viver nel fango
[18b] Di seguir falso duce
[18c] E poi ch'a mortal rischio
[18d] Reggami per pietà

TEXT

Io, che l'età solea viver nel fango
Oggi, mutato il cor da quel, ch'i soglio,
D'ogni immondo pensier mi purgo e spoglio,
E'l mio lungo fallir correggo e piango:

Di seguir falso duce mi rimango;
A te mi dono; ad ogni altro mi toglio.
Né rotta nave mai partí da scoglio,
Si pentita del mar, com'io rimango.

E poi ch'a mortal rischio è gita invano,
E senza frutto i cari giorni ha spesi
Questa mia vita, in porto omai l'accolgo.

Reggami per pietà tua santa mano,
Padre del ciel, che poich'a te mi volgo,
Tanto t'adorerò, quant'io t'offesi.

[(a) Up to now living in mire, today with heart changed I purge myself of every unclean thought; I purify myself, crying out: (b) I renounce fealty to a false leader; I give myself to Thee, keeping myself from all others; no shattered ship lifted from the rocks is as repentant as I. (c) And since mortality is a risky voyage (and my life has used up valuable time fruitlessly), I welcome it back in port. (d) Extend to me your holy hand, heav-

enly Father, now that I turn to you: I shall worship Thee as much as I have offended Thee.]

    The author is Giovanni della Casa. Caccini sets this sonnet, No. XVII of della Casa's *Rime*, in four *partes*; see Baldassar Castiglione, Giovanni della Casa, *Opere*, ed. Giuseppe Prezzolini (Milan, Rome: Rizzoli, 1937), p. 647; [18a] = lines 1-4, [18b] = 5-8, [18c] = 9-11, and [18d] = 12-14.

MUSIC

Ms. versions:

(None located)

Nuove musiche (1614), pp. 33-6 (*recte* 29-32):

    m. 4, voice: The last three beats are ♫ ♫ ♪ ♪ (unbeamed).

    m. 21, voice: The second F is natural.

    m. 28, voice: The second E is natural.

    m. 29, voice: Only the first F is sharp.

    m. 30, voice: The second F is natural.

    m. 31, voice: The second F is natural.

    m. 44, voice: Only the first E is flat.

    m. 50, voice: The second F is natural.

    m. 59, voice: Only the first F is sharp.

    m. 67, voice: The second E is natural.

    m. 69, voice: The second F is natural.

    m. 70, voice: The second F is natural.

    m. 71, voice: Only the first F is sharp.

    m. 71, bass:

    m. 100, voice: The second E is natural.

    m. 103, voice: The second F is natural.

[19a] Deh chi d'alloro
[19b] Già non l'allaccia

TEXT

Deh chi d'alloro
Mi fa ghirland' al crine,
Pur mi god'io vittorioso al fine
Il mio tesoro
La mia nemic' altera
È pur mia prigioniera.

Quell'alma dura
Ch'a miei sospiri ardenti
Rassembrò giel che 'n rigid'Alpe ai venti
S'innaspra, e 'ndura
Stilla in pianto d'amore
All'amoroso ardore.

Già non l'allaccia
D'aspra caten' il ferro,
Cortese vincitor tra le mie braccia
La guardo e serro,
Nè voglio altro tributo
Che 'l cor a me dovuto.

Ben duro scoglio
In van l'onda percuote,
Ma in cor di donna un'ostinato orgoglio
Durar non puote;
Troppo de' veri amanti
Ponno i sospiri e i pianti.

[(a) Over her who now has garlanded my locks with laurel I am finally victorious: my treasure—my proud enemy!—is now my prisoner. That harsh soul, which hardened in my ardent sighs as alpine ice hardens in the winds, now melts into tears of love. (b) Now no harsh iron chain need bind her: a kind conqueror, I hold her in my arms; I gaze at her, and squeeze, and no other spoils do I wish than her heart which is due me. Although waves beat in vain against a hard rock, pride in a woman's heart cannot resist the sighs and tears of true lovers.]

The author is Ottavio Rinuccini. Caccini sets as a double aria stanzas 4 and 2 (= [19a]) and 5 and 6 (= [19b]) of the six-stanza poem "O voi ch'in pianto"; see *Poesie del Sr Ottavio Rinuccini* (Florence: I Giunti, 1622), pp. 187-8. Each stanza of the poem is of six lines, in *quinario*, *settenario*, and *endecasillabo* verses, with the rhyme and meter scheme a^5 b^7 b^{11} a^5 c^7 c^7.

MUSIC

Ms. versions:

(None located)

Nuove musiche (1614), pp. 37-9 (*recte* 33-5):

m. 21, voice: The second beat is

(unbeamed).

m. 26, voice: The last half of the measure is

(unbeamed).

m. 27, voice: The first beat is

(unbeamed).

m. 28, voice: The first half of the measure is

(unbeamed).

m. 43, voice: Only the first B is flat.

m. 46, voice: The second beat is

(unbeamed).

[20] Mentre che fra doglie e pene

TEXT

Mentre che fra doglie e pene
Nutr'il cor spirto di speme
Trass'i dì lieti e contenti
Ne gli affanni, e ne i tormenti
Or di spem' in tutto privo
Di dolor mi pasco e vivo.

Mentre che dolce mia vita
Non ti spiacque darmi aita
Sai ben tu che strali, e foco,
Mi fur sempre festa, e gioco;
Hor non posso, il vo pur dire,
Star nel foco e non morire.

Mentre che cruda e severa
Pur ti mostri, e vuoi ch'io pera,
Mi morrò nè tu potrai
Darmi aita oimè, che fai?
Vorrai tu ch'a si gran torto,
Chi t'adora resti morto?

Mentre che tra pace e guerra
Viveran gli amanti in terra,
Sia pur fera, e sia crudele
Ti sarò servo fedele
Che se ben tal hor mi doglio
Non per questo a te mi toglio.

[(1) As a hopeless heart feeds on pain, turning happy days into grief and torment, so, devoid of hope, do I feed and live on grief. (2) While, sweetheart, it displeases you not to help me, you well know that arrows and fire were always fun and games to me. But now, I must say, I cannot remain in the flames and not perish. (3) While you are cruel and harsh, and wish me to perish, with my death you'll not be able to help me: ah, then, what will you do? Do you wish so wrongfully that he who adores you be dead? (4) While earthly lovers will live amidst peace and war, be then beastly and cruel; I shall remain your faithful servant: even if sometimes I complain, not for that reason do I tear myself away.]

The author is perhaps Ottavio Rinuccini: a version concording perfectly with that of *Nuove musiche* (1614) is in Florence, Biblioteca Nazionale, Codex Palatino 250, fol. [11]-[11ᵛ], amidst other poems securely attributable to Rinuccini. The poem is a canzonet in four six-line stanzas, each entirely in *ottonario* verses, with the rhyme scheme *a a b b c c*.

MUSIC

Ms. versions:

1. Florence, Bibl. Naz., Ms. Magl. XIX.66, fol. [61ᵛ]-[62].
2. Brussels, Bibl. du Cons., Ms. 704, pp. 101-2.

Nuove musiche (1614), p. 39 (*recte* 35):

    m. 14, voice: The second C is natural.

    mm. 33-34, bass: The hemiola cadence is indicated in black notation: ● ● ● .

[21] Non ha 'l ciel cotanti lumi

TEXT

Non ha 'l ciel cotanti lumi,
Tante still' e mari e fiumi,
Non l'April gigli e viole,
Tanti raggi non ha il Sole,
Quant'ha doglie e pen'ogni hora
Cor gentil che s'innamora.

Penar lungo e gioir corto,
Morir vivo e viver morto,
Spem' incerta e van desire,
Mercè poca a gran languire,
Falsi risi e veri pianti
È la vita degli amanti.

Neve al sol e nebbia al vento,
E d'Amor gioia e contento,
Degli affanni e delle pene
Ahi che 'l fin già mai non viene,
Giel di morte estingue ardore
Ch'in un'alma accende amore.

Ben soll'io che 'l morir solo
Può dar fine al mio gran duolo,
Nè di voi già mi dogl'io
Del mio stato acerbo e rio;
Sol' Amor tiranno accuso,
Occhi belli, e voi ne scuso.

[(1) The heavens have no more stars, the seas and rivers no more droplets, April no more lilies and violets, the sun no more rays, than has a lover pain and grief. (2) Long suffering and brief pleasure, living death and deathly life, uncertain hope and vain desires, merciless languor, false laughs and real tears—this is the lot of lovers. (3) Snow in the sun and fog in the wind, joy in love but pain and grief, too. Ah! let the end never come, when the chill of death extinguishes the fire lit by love. (4) Though I know well that only death can end my grief, I never grieve on your account for my bitter lot: only Love do I accuse, my beauty; you I excuse.]

    The author is Ottavio Rinuccini; see *Poesie del Sr Ottavio Rinuccini* (Florence: I Giunti, 1622), p. 189. A manuscript version (unattributed) is in Florence, Biblioteca Nazionale, Codex Palatino 250, fol. 12-12^v. The poem is a canzonet in eight six-line stanzas, each of which is entirely in *ottonario* verses, with the rhyme scheme *a a b b c c*.

MUSIC

Ms. versions:

1. Florence, Bibl. Naz., Ms. Magl. XIX.66, fol. [73^v]-[74].
2. Florence, Cons., Ms. Barbera, fol. [20^v]-[21].
3. Brussels, Bibl. du Cons., Ms. 704, pp. 79-80.

Nuove musiche (1614), p. 40 (*recte* 36):

    m. 6, voice: The second E is natural.

    m. 7, voice: The syllable "ma-" is laid under the second C.

    m. 16, bass: Both notes are C's.

    mm. 37-8, bass: The hemiola is indicated in black notation: ● ● ● .

[22] Amor ch'attendi

TEXT

Amor ch'attendi,
Amor che fai?
Su, che non prendi
Gli strali omai;
Amor vendetta,
Amor saetta
Quel cor ch'altero
Sdegna 'l tuo impero.

O' pompa, ò gloria,
O' spoglie altere,
Nobil vittoria
S'Amor la fere;
Amor ardisci,
Amor ferisci,
Amor et odi
Qual havrà i lodi?

Amor possente
Amor cortese
Dirà la gente
Pur arse e prese
Quella crudele,
Che, di querele
Vaga, e di pianti,
Schernia gli amanti.

Quel cor superbo
Langue e sospira,
Quel viso acerbo
Pietate spira.
Fatti duoi fiumi
Quei crudi lumi,
Pur versan fore
Pianto d'amore.

Se cruda e ria
Negò mercede,
Humile e pia
Mercede hor chiede.

O' face, ò strale,
Alta immortale,
Che fia che scampi
Si 'l giaccio avvampi.

Dall'alto cielo
Fulmina Giove,
L'Arcier di Delo
Saette piove,
Ma lo stral d'oro
S'orni d'alloro
Che di possanza
Ogni altro avanza.

[(1) Why do you delay, Love? Why have you not read-
ied your darts? Vengeance, Love! Pierce that heart
which haughtily denies your hegemony. (2) O pomp,
o glory, o proud spoils! 'Twill be a noble victory if
Love wounds her. Should Love burn and batter, which
—Love or Hate—will get the glory? (3) People will say
that powerful Love, kind Love, has burned and captured that cruel one who, enjoying quarrels and laments, sneers at lovers. (4) That proud heart lan-
guishes, that dour face now breathes pity. Those cruel
eyes are become two rivers that pour out tears of love.
(5) If it cruelly denied mercy before, now it humbly
asks mercy. O fiery dart, who can escape your firing
their ice? (6) From heaven on high Jupiter hurls thun-
derbolts, the archer of Delos [Apollo] rains down arrows. But let the golden arrow [of Cupid] that sur-
passes all in strength be crowned with laurel.]

The author is probably Ottavio Rinuccini: a version
(unattributed) concording perfectly with that of *Nuove
musiche* (1614) is in Florence, Biblioteca Nazionale,
Codex Palatino 250, fol. [25]-[26ᵛ], amidst other poems
securely attributable to Rinuccini. Bianca Becherini,
*Catalogo dei manoscritti musicali della Biblioteca Nazionale
di Firenze* (Kassel, Basel: Bärenreiter, 1959), pp. 8-9, at-
tributes the poem to Gabriello Chiabrera, but without
documentation. The poem is a canzonet in six eight-
line stanzas, each entirely in *quinario* verses, with the
rhyme scheme *a b a b c c d d*.

MUSIC

Ms. versions:

1. Brussels, Bibl. du Cons., Ms. 704, pp. 181-2.
2. Florence, Bibl. Naz., Ms. Magl. XIX.25, fol. [20ᵛ]-
   [21].

Editions:

1. *La Flora*, ed. Knud Jeppesen (Copenhagen: W.
   Hansen, 1949), III: 4.

Nuove musiche (1614), p. 41 (*recte* 37):

m. 2, bass: The F is natural.
mm. 21-22, bass: The hemiola is indicated in black
   notation: • • • .

[23] O piante, o selve ombrose

TEXT

O piante, o selve ombrose,
O valli, o rive erbose,
Fioriti colli,
Fiorite piagge,
Erbette molli,
Fere selvagge,
Fugace e fresco rio,
Pietà del morir mio.

Soffrir tanti martiri,
Nutrir tanti sospiri,
Versare stille
Da gli occhi fore
A mille a mille
Più non può 'l core:
Può solo e vuol morire
Pe 'l suo dolor finire.

Già vissi nel tormento
E nel dolor contento,
E i sospir miei
E'l pianto amaro
Sparso per lei
Già mi fu caro;
Hor m'è si aspro e forte
Ch'io bramo la mia morte.

Per donna ch'è si bella,
Che ne rassembra stella,
Lieto penai
Quando mercede
Trovar pensai
A la mia fede;
Ma hor ch'io non lo spero
Accuso il mio pensiero.

Haver qualche pietade
Credeï tanta beltade,
Che non inferno,
Ma paradiso,
S'io ben discerne,
Sembra quel viso,
E'l cor apersi stolto,
A i colpi del bel volto.

Crescendo a poco a poco
Venuto è poi quel foco
Che 'l dolce sguardo
M'avventò al seno,
Si ch'io tutt' ardo
Venendo meno,
Nè lasso più speranza
Di refrigerio avanza.

[(1) O plants and shady woods, o valleys and mossy
riverbanks, flowering hills and dales, tender shoots of
grass, wild beasts, fleeting fresh brook: have mercy on
me, dying. (2) To suffer such martyrdom, to house
such hopes, to shed tears by the thousands—no more

can my heart stand it; it can, and wishes only to, die to end its grief. (3) I once lived in torment, happy in grief, and my sighs and bitter plaint for her were sweet to me. Now it is so terribly harsh that I long for death. (4) For a woman so lovely that she resembles a star I cheerfully suffered, so long as I thought to find pity for my fidelity; but now, without hope, I begrudge my thought. (5) I thought such beauty would have some pity, that that face resembled not hell but paradise. And my heart was fooled by her beauteous glances. (6) The sweet look she hurled at my breast inflamed it bit by bit—so much that, all afire, I have no more hope of cooling relief.]

The author is perhaps Ottavio Rinuccini; the poem is thus attributed by Francesco Trucchi, *Poesie italiane inedite di dugento autori . . .* (Prato, 1846-7), IV: 117. The poem is a canzonet in eleven eight-line stanzas, each in *quinario* and *settenario* verses, with the rhyme and meter scheme $a^7\ a^7\ b^5\ c^5\ b^5\ c^5\ d^7\ d^7$.

MUSIC

Ms. versions:

1. Florence, Bibl. Naz., Ms. Magl. XIX.66, fol. [77^v]-[78].
2. Brussels, Bibl. du Cons., Ms. 704, pp. 99-100.

Editions:

1. (Stanza 1 only; bass not realized, barring as in original): in Lorenzo Bianconi, "Caccini e il manierismo musicale," *Chigiana* XXV (1968): 33.

Nuove musiche (1614), p. 42 (*recte* 38):

mm. 10-11, bass: The hemiola is indicated in black notation: ♩ ♩ ♪♪ .

[24] Tu ch'hai le penne Amore

TEXT

Tu ch'hai le penne Amore
E sai spiegarle a volo,
Deh muovi ratto un volo
Fin là dov'è 'l mio core.
E se non sai la via,
Co' miei sospir t'invia.

Va pur ch'il troverrai
Tra 'l velo e 'l bianco seno,
O tra 'l dolce sereno
De' luminosi rai,
O tra bei nodi d'oro
Del mio dolce tesoro.

Vanne lusinga, e prega
Perchè dal bel soggiorno
Faccia il mio cor ritorno,
E se'l venir pur niega,
Rivolto al nostro sole,
Digli cotai parole:

Quel tuo fedele amante,
Tra lieta amica gente,
Vive mesto e dolente,
E col tristo sembiante
D'ogni allegrezza spento
Turba l'altrui contento.

Di che fra 'l canto e 'l riso
Spargo sospir di foco,
Che fra 'l diletto e'l gioco
Non mai sereno il viso,
Che d'alma e di cor privo
Stommi fra morto e vivo.

S'entro alle tepide onde
D'Arno, fra lauri e faggi
Fuggon gli estivi raggi,
Io, su l'ombrose sponde
O 'n su l'ardente arena,
Resto carco di pena.

Se dal sassoso fondo
Il crin stillante e molle
Orcheno, il capo e i stolle
Di preda il sen fecondo
Ove ognun un correr' miro
A pena un guardo io giro.

Mentre per piagge e colli
Seguon fugaci fiere
Le cacciatrici fiere;
Lass'io con gli occhi molli
Hor del cesto, hor del resco
L'onda piangendo accresco.

Non degli augei volanti
Miro le prede e i voli
Sol perchè mi consoli
Versar sospiri e pianti—
Ma dì ch'io non vorrei
Far noti i dolor' miei.

Amor cortese impetra
Ch'a me torni il cor mio
O ch'ella il mandi, ond'io
Più non sembri huom di pietra
Nè più con tristo aspetto
Turbi l'altrui diletto.

Ma se per mia ventura
Del suo tornar dubbiosa
Mandarlo a me non osa,
Amor prometti e giura,
Che suo fu sempre, e sia
Il core a l'alma mia.

[(1) You, Love, who have wings and know how to spread them in flight, ah! fly quickly where my heart is; and if you do not know the way, follow my sighs. (2) Go: you will find it in the veiled white breast of my dear treasure, or in the sweetness of her bright glances, or in her golden locks. (3) Go lure her, and beg that from its sweet sojourn she allow my heart to return. And if she refuses to let it come back, tell her this: (4) "Your faithful lover lives sorrowful and grieving among others who are happy, and with sad and joyless mien disturbs their happiness." (5) Say that 'midst song and laughter I scatter burning sighs; that among pleasures and pastimes never is my visage serene; that, deprived of heart and soul, I am at the point of death. (6) [Say that] whereas sunbeams play on the warm waves of the Arno, flitting among laurels and beeches, I remain grief-laden on the shady banks or the burning sand. (7) [Say that] if Orcheno emerges from the rocky bottom, hair dripping wet, blouse full of booty, and everyone else rushes to look, I give hardly a glance. (8) [Say that] while o'er hill and dale proud huntresses follow fleeting wild beasts, I remain weeping, and from my basket the wave of tears increases. (9) [Say that] I watch not the flying prey swooping down from the heights; that my only consolation is to pour forth sighs and plaints. But say also that I do not wish my grief to be known. (10) Kind Love, beseech her to give back my heart, so that I no longer seem a soul of stone nor disturb others' pleasure with sad mien. (11) But if by unhappy chance she dares not give it back, o Love, swear to her that my heart was, and is still, hers.]

The author is probably Ottavio Rinuccini: versions (unattributed) concording excellently with that of *Nuove musiche* (1614) are in Florence, Biblioteca Nazionale, Codex Palatino 249 (attributed as a whole to Rinuccini), fol. 111-12ᵛ, and Codex Palatino 250, fol. 1-3. The poem is a canzonet in eleven six-line stanzas, each entirely in *settenario* verses, with the rhyme scheme *a b b a c c.*

MUSIC

Ms. versions:

(None located)

Nuove musiche (1614), p. 42 (*recte* 39):

mm. 30-1, bass: The hemiola is indicated in black notation: ● ● ● .

[25] Al fonte, al prato

TEXT

Al fonte, al prato,
Al bosco, a l'ombra,
Al fresco fiato
Ch'il caldo sgombra,
Pastor correte;
Ciascun ch'a sete,
Ciascun ch'è stanco
Ripos' il fianco.

Fugga la noia,
Fugga il dolore,
Sol riso e gioia,
Sol caro amore.
Nosco soggiorni

Ne' lieti giorni.
Nè s'odan mai
Querele o lai.

Ma dolce canto
Di vaghi uccelli
Pe 'l verde manto
Degli arbuscelli
Risuoni sempre
Con nuovi tempre,
Mentre ch'a l'onde
Ecco risponde.

E mentre alletta
Quanto più puote
La giovinetta
Con rozze note
Il sonno dolce,
Ch'il caldo molce,
E noi pian piano
Con lei cantiano.

[(1) To the spring, to the meadow, to the woods, to the shade, to the fresh breeze that disperses the heat, hasten, o shepherds! Let him who is thirsty, let him who is weary, rest. (2) Away with boredom, away with grief! Let only laughter, joy, and love be among us. In these happy days, never let there be heard complaints or laments. (3) Rather let there resound with new timbres the sweet song of pretty birds through the green mantle of the saplings, while echoes call back and forth to the waves. (4) And while the damsel charms as best she can with rough notes the sweet sleep that soothes the heat, let us softly sing with her.]

The poem is by Francesco Cini (private communication from Tim Carter, University of Birmingham, via Nigel Fortune). It is a canzonet in four eight-line stanzas, each entirely in *quinario* verses, with the rhyme scheme *a b a b c c d d.*

MUSIC

Ms. versions:

1. Florence, Bibl. Naz., Ms. Magl. XIX.66, fol. [65ᵛ]-[66].
2. Florence, Cons., Ms. Barbera, fol. [17].
3. Brussels, Bibl. du Cons., Ms. 704, pp. 87-8.

Editions:

1. *La Flora*, ed. Knud Jeppesen (Copenhagen: W. Hansen, 1949), III: 6.

Nuove musiche (1614), p. 44 (*recte* 40):

m. 1, bass: The first note is dotted.

[26] Aur'amorosa

TEXT

Aur'amorosa
Che dolcemente spiri

Al bel mattin mentre sorge l'aurora,
Deh spir' ogni ora.

Portane teco
Dal celeste sereno
Di perle un vago e rugiadoso nembo
A i fiori in grembo.

E teco insieme
Veng' Amor, Gioco e Riso;
L' Hore, le Gratie e le dotte sorelle
Venghino anch'elle.

Sgombrine omai
L'ardir ch'incenerisce
Il monte e 'l piano, e fa ch'al tuo valore
Respiri il core.

Aprirne un giorno
Viè più che mai tranquillo
Si ch'ogni spirto tua mercè ravvive
In queste rive.

[(1) Amorous breeze that sweetly blows in the morning as dawn breaks, oh blow forever! (2) Bring with you from the heavens, to the flowers in our laps, a lovely, dewy shower of pearls. (3) And let come with you Love, Fun, and Laughter—also the Hours, the Graces, and their learned sisters. (4) Now snuff out the fire that reduces the mountain and plain to ashes, and let hearts breathe as only you can. (5) Let dawn a day more tranquil than ever, so that every soul on these banks is revived by your favors.]

The author is unidentified. The poem is a canzonet in five four-line stanzas, each in *quinario, settenario,* and *endecasillabo* verses, with the rhyme and meter scheme $a^5 \, b^7 \, c^{11} \, c^5$.

MUSIC

Ms. versions:

1. Florence, Cons., Ms. Barbera, fol. [24].

Editions:

1. *La Flora,* ed. Knud Jeppesen (Copenhagen: W. Hansen, 1949), III: 5.

Nuove musiche (1614), p. 45 (*recte* 41):

m. 2, bass: The figure "4" is printed upside-down and reversed.

[27] O che felice giorno

TEXT

O che felice giorno,
O che lieto ritorno,
Ravviva il cor già spento.
Quanta dolcezza sento!
O mia luce, o mia vita,
O mia gioia infinita.

Ecco 'l mio ben ritorna,
E queste rive adorna;
Eccone lieto il giro
Del bel guardo ch'io miro.
Occhi belli, occhi cari,
Occhi del sol più chiari.

Hor ben prov'io nel petto
Non dolor' ma diletto;
Torna la chiara e bella
Mia rilucente stella,
Torna il Sol, torna l'aura,
Torna chi mi restaura.

Dolce hor mia vita rende
Quel Dio ch'i cori accende;
Amor che l'havea tolto
Hor mi rende il bel volto.
Il mio cor, il mio bene,
Il mio conforto e speme.

[(1) O what a joyous day! O what a happy return! A spent heart is revived: what sweetness I feel! O light of my life, o infinite joy of mine! (2) Behold, my love returns and adorns these banks. Behold the happiness of that glance I observe. O lovely, sweet eyes, eyes brighter than the sun! (3) Now indeed I feel in my breast not grief but pleasure. My bright, beautiful, twinkling star has returned. The sun, the dawn, everything life-giving to me has returned. (4) Now that god who inflames hearts makes my life sweet; Love, who used to keep it from me, now gives me your lovely face: my sweetheart, my love, my comfort and hope.]

The author is unidentified. The poem is a canzonet in four six-line stanzas, each entirely in *settenario* verses, with the rhyme scheme *a a b b c c.*

MUSIC

Ms. versions:

1. Florence, Bibl. Naz., Ms. Magl. XIX.66, fol. [70ᵛ]-[71].
2. Brussels, Bibl. du Cons., Ms. 704, pp. 93-4.

Editions:

1. *La Flora,* ed. Knud Jeppesen (Copenhagen: W. Hansen, 1949), III: 3.

Nuove musiche (1614), p. 46 (*recte* 42):

m. 1, bass: The first note is dotted.
m. 8, voice: The second E is natural.

[28] Dalla porta d'oriente

TEXT

Dalla porta d'oriente
Lampeggiando in ciel usciva
E le nubi coloriva
L'alba candida e lucente,

E per l'aure rugiadose
Apria gigli e spargea rose.

Quand'al nostr'almo terreno
Distendendo i dolci lampi
Vide aprir su i nostri campi
D'altra luce altro sereno;
E portando altr'alba il giorno
Dileguar la notte intorno.

Ch'a sgombrar l'oscuro velo
Più soave e vezzosetta,
Una vaga giovinetta
Accendea le rose in cielo,
E di fiamme porporine
Feria l'aure matutine.

Era il crine a l'aria sparso
Onde l'oro apria suo riso,
E la neve del bel viso
Dolce porpora havea sparso,
E su'l collo alabastrino
Biancheggiava il gelsomino.

Da le labbra innamorate,
Muov' Amor con novi strali,
E di perle orientali
Se ne gian l'alme fregiate,
Et ardeva i cor meschini
Dolce foco di rubini.

Di due splendide facelle
Tanta fiamma discendea,
Che la terra intorno ardea
Et ardeva in ciel le stelle;
E se'l sole usciva fuora,
Havrebb'arso il sole ancora.

Dov'il piè con vago giro,
Dove l'occhio amor partia,
Ogni passo un fiore apria,
Ogni sguardo un bel zaffiro;
E s'udia più dolc'e lento
Mormorar con l'acqua il vento.

L'alba in ciel s'adira e vede
Che le toglie il suo splendore
Questa nova alba d'amore,
E già volge in dietro il piede,
E stillar d'amaro pianto
Già comincia il roseo manto.

[(1) From the eastern gate came bright shining dawn, sparkling in the heavens, and it tinted the clouds and with dewy breezes opened the lilies and scattered roses. (2) Then, as it shed its sweet rays over our blessed realm, it saw appear among us the brightness of another light: daylight brought another dawn to dispel the darkness. (3) To clear the veil of darkness, a sweeter, more charming and lovely damsel illuminated the pink clouds of heaven, and with purple flames fired the morning breezes. (4) From her tresses, loose in the breeze, gold took its laughter; and her snowy white cheeks were dappled with purple; and on her alabaster neck jasmine glistened. (5) From her amorous lips Love issued with fresh darts; spirits were decorated with exotic pearls, and a sweet ruby fire lit up miserable hearts. (6) Such flame came from her two bright little torches that the earth caught fire, as did the stars in heaven; and had the sun come out, it too would have burst into flame. (7) Wherever her foot trod, wherever her glance shone with love, a flower opened at every step, a zephyr arose with every look; and one heard, sweet and low, the murmur of breezes as well as of water. (8) The heavenly dawn is angry to see how this new dawn of love robs her of her splendor; she retraces her steps and already from her rosy mantle begins to shed bitter tears.]

The author is given as Maria Menadori in Francesco Trucchi, *Poesie italiane inedite di dugento autori . . .* (Prato, 1846-7), IV: 93. The poem is a canzonet in eight six-line stanzas, each entirely in *ottonario* verses, with the rhyme scheme *a b b a c c*.

MUSIC

Ms. versions:

1. Florence, Bibl. Naz., Ms. Magl. XIX.66, fol. [22ᵛ].
2. Florence, Cons., Ms. Barbera, fol. [23ᵛ].
3. Brussels, Bibl. du Cons., Ms. 704, pp. 191-2.
4. Tenbury, St. Michael's College, Ms. 1018, fol. 42.

Nuove musiche (1614):

Throughout: This song must be almost entirely rebarred to reveal the play between 8 and 4 meters. The original barring is indicated in the edition proper.

[29] Con le luci d'un bel ciglio

TEXT

Con le luci d'un bel ciglio,
Co'l vermiglio
Di due guance alme rosate,
Con due labbra di rubini,
Con bei crini,
Mi combatte empia beltate.

Ad ogni hor mi dona assalto,
O che in alto
Sproni Febo i suoi destrieri
O ch'in mar' sue fiamme chiuda
E la cruda
Chiama in campo i miei pensieri.

Ah da lei fuggir lontano
Lasso in vano.
Il sudor per me s'impiega
Perch'Amor par che l'a'mpiumi
Si sui fiumi,
E su'l mar' le insegna spiega.

Hor chi porge alcun' ahita
A mia vita?
Se fuggir non ho possanza,
Ch'io contrasti alcun non dica
Tal nemica
Soverchiar non è possanza.

[(1) A pitiless beauty battles me with the lights of her lovely brow, with the vermilion of two divinely rosy cheeks, with two ruby lips, with beautiful tresses. (2) All the time she assaults me. O that on high Phoebus would spur on his warhorses! O that he would snuff out her flames in the sea and that the cruel one would hear my thoughts. (3) Ah! useless to flee far from her. Now I must labor so that Love will feather her wings: up, up, ye waters! and spread out your signs on the sea. (4) Who will now lend my life help? Even if I am powerless to flee, let no one say I have not the power to overcome such an opponent if I try.]

The author is unidentified. The poem is a canzonet in four six-line stanzas, each in *quadernario* and *ottonario* verses, with the rhyme and meter scheme a^8 a^4 b^8 c^8 c^4 b^8.

MUSIC

Ms. versions:

1. Florence, Cons., Ms. Barbera, fol. [73^v].
2. Brussels, Bibl. du Cons., Ms. 704, pp. 215-16.

Nuove musiche (1614), p. 48 (*recte* 44):

Throughout: This song must be almost entirely re-barred. See the comment on [28].
mm. 4-5, voice:

m. 6, voice: The last note is an eighth-note.

NUOVE MUSICHE E NUOVA MANIERA DI SCRIVERLE
(1614)

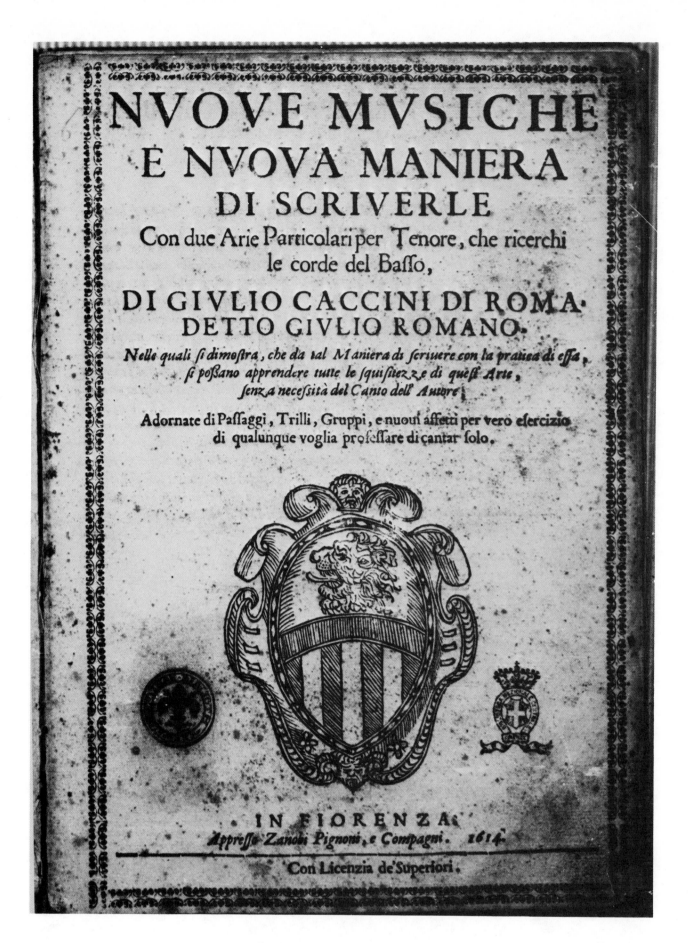

Plate I. Title page of *Nuove musiche* (1614).
(Courtesy, Biblioteca Nazionale Centrale, Florence)

NEW COMPOSITIONS
AND A NEW WAY
OF WRITING THEM OUT

With two special airs for tenor, who explores
the bass range

BY GIULIO CACCINI OF ROME
CALLED GIULIO ROMANO

In which it is shown that with this new way, and practice in it,
all the delicacies of this art can be learned
without having to hear the composer sing;

Adorned with diminutions, tremolos, trills, and new effects
for the thorough training of anyone wishing to be expert in solo song.

IN FLORENCE.
At Zanobi Pignoni & Co. 1614.

With permission of [the] authorities.

AL MOLTO ILLVSTRE SIGNOR PIERO
FALCONIERI MIO SIG.

HANNO *costumato spesse volte coloro che appresero qualche arte,*
ò disciplina da alcuno, o che da alcuno ebbero occasione di appren-
derla, di offerirle le prime fatiche, che intorno a cotal arte, o disci
plina hanno fatte, e mandato fuori, mostrando per questa maniera
in verso di quello alcun segno di debita gratitudine; ma riguar-
dando io quanto grande sia l'antico obbligo che io tengo alla memo-
ria del Sig. Paolo Falconieri, che mi consigliò in mia giouentù a gli studi della Musica, e mi spinse, e mi sforzò per dir così con l'aiuto de' suoi fauori e della sua protez-
zione ad impiegarmiui lungamente, offertrè à V.S. suo maggior figliuolo non le pri-
mizie, ma quelle considerazioni, che hò messo insieme intorno al modo del ben cantare, da potersi apprendere ogni sua squisitezza dà gli scritti dopo l'osseruazione di
molt'anni non solamente con l'esercitar continuamente nel canto me stesso, e la mia
moglie, e le mie figliuole, ma con l'hauer sentito i maggior cantanti huomini, e
donne, che in Italia, e fuori d'Italia sono stati nei termine di cinquant'ãni, ò sono al presente, potrà V.S. conoscere che l'ossequio mio in verso la casa sua cominciato ne gli
anni della mia fanciullezza, e peruenuto sino à quelli della vecchiaia per far il medesimo sino al fine di quei pochi che mi possono auanzare desiderando in tanto à V.S.
somma felicità e baciandole le mani di Casa. il dì 18. d'Agosto, 1614.

Di V.S. molto Illustre.

Seruitore affezzionatissimo, & obbligatiss.

Giulio Caccini di Roma.

Plate II. Dedication page of *Nuove musiche* (1614).
(Courtesy, Biblioteca Nazionale Centrale, Florence)

TO MY MOST ILLUSTRIOUS LORD, SIGNOR PIERO FALCONIERI

Those who have learned an art or discipline from someone, or have been led by someone to learn it, have often dedicated to that person the first efforts in such an art or discipline that they have produced and made public, thus giving the person an indication of their proper gratitude. However, I recognize how great is the long-standing debt that I owe to the memory of Sig[nor] Paolo Falconieri, who advised me in my youth to take up musical studies and with the aid of his favors and protection urged me—indeed, forced me, so to speak—to devote myself to them for a long time. Thus I shall offer to Y[our] E[xcellency], his eldest son, not the first fruits but those [ripe] conclusions that I have reached concerning the manner of good singing, [presented] in such a way as to enable one to learn its every nicety from the written [notes], after [my] many years of study not only by continually practicing the art of song myself (as have also my wife and daughters) but by having listened to the greatest singers of the past fifty years, both male and female, in Italy and elsewhere. Y[our] E[xcellency] may thus realize that my respect for your family, which had its origin in my boyhood, has continued into my old age, and will so to the end of the brief time that is left to me. Hoping in the meantime for Y[our] E[xcellency]'s greatest happiness, and offering my highest regards, [written] at home, 18 August 1614,

Y[our] most illustrious E[xcellency]'s

most affectionate and obliging servant,

Giulio Caccini of Rome.

A DISCRETI LETTORI.

MOLTI anni auanti, che io mettessi alcuna delle mie opere di musica, per vna voce sola, alla stampa, se ne eran vedute fuora molte altre mie, fatte in diuersi tempi, & occasioni, delle quali furono più note, la musica, che io feci nella fauola della Dafne del Sig. Ottauio Rinuccini, rappresentata in casa del Sig. Iacopo Corsi d'onorata memoria à quest' Altezze Serenissime, & altri Prencipi; mà le prime, che io stampassi furon le musiche fatte l'anno 1600. nella fauola dell'Euridice, opera del medesimo autore; e furon le prime, che si ve desser date in luce in Italia da qualunque compositore di tale stile à vna voce sola; diedi appresso fuore l'anno 1601. quelle, che io intitolai le nuoue musiche, e con quelle pubblicai vn discorso, nel quale si contiene (s'io non erro) tutto quello, che può desiderare chi professi di cantar solo, e veduto al presente quanto l'vni uersale abbracci, e gradisca questa mia maniera di cantar solo, la quale io scriuo giustamente, come si canta, quanto sia preferito à gli altri, per lo spaccio, che di tal'opre hanno hauto gli stampatori; e considerato quanto, oltre al cantar solo sia stata gradita la maniera delle musiche de'cori di dette fauole, e l'inuenzione di essi, e d'altre fauole, fatte poi, doue parimente hò fatto diuerse arie secondo che richiedeuano i diuersi affetti di tali cori, chiare & armoniose, mi son resoluto à stampar di nuouo quest'altre mie, alcune delle quali sono scritte nell'istessa manie ra, che conuiene, che siano cantate, hauendo segnato sopra la parte, che canta, e trilli, e gruppi, & altri nuoui affetti non più veduti per le stampe, con passag gi più proprij per la voce, ne i quali passaggi per hora non hò voluto mostrare al tra varietà in essi essendomi questi parsi a bastanza per vero esercizio in que st'arte, non hauendo hauuto riguardo à replicar più volte i medesimi potendo esser questi scalà ad altri più difficili, come ad altro tempo si mostrerà; alcune ce n'hò inserte, le quali tal'hora cantano in voce di tenore, e tal'hora di basso con passaggi più propri per amendue le parti, e queste per vso di chi hauesse talento dalla natura di ricercare gli estremi di esse voci, essendo necessario in detta par te di basso nelle simiminime, e crome col punto, che discendano per grado, trillarne or l'vna, & ora l'altra, per darle maggior grazia, forza, e spirito, e per dirsi brauura, e ardire, che più si ricerca in detta parte, e nella quale vi si richie de assai meno l'affetto, che nella parte del tenore; in quanto alla misura, ò lar ghezza da osseruarsi in dette arie secondo che è maggiore la grauità da vsarsi, conforme à gli affetti delle parole, e altri mouimenti della voce piu nell'vna, che nell'altra parte, io me ne rimetto al giudizio del cantante, & insieme al mio

✤ 2   stam-

Plate III. First page of preface of *Nuove musiche* (1614).
(Courtesy, Biblioteca Nazionale Centrale, Florence)

TO [MY] DISCRIMINATING READERS

Many years before I had any of my music for solo voice published, many works that I had produced at various times and on different occasions were heard publicly, of which the most noted was the music that I did for the tale of Dafne by Sig[nor] Ottavio Rinuccini, staged in the house of Sig[nor] Jacopo Corsi, who is remembered with respect by our Most Serene Highnesses and other princes. But the first that I had printed was the music I composed in 1600 for the tale of Euridice, a work by the same author; and that was the first music in such a style for solo voice to be published in Italy by any composer. I next brought out, in 1601 [1602, new style], those [pieces] I called *Le nuove musiche,* and with them I published an essay in which is to be found, if I am not mistaken, everything needed by anyone who wishes to master solo song.

Seeing how by now everyone has taken up with pleasure my style of solo singing, which I write out exactly as it is sung, and how (judging by the sales made by publishers of such works) it is preferred to others', and considering also how much appreciated, besides the solo songs, have been the style and the inventiveness of the choral music of the above-mentioned tales [*La Dafne, L'Euridice*] and others I composed thereafter, for which likewise I composed various bright and harmonious airs as required by the different moods of such choruses, I have decided to publish now some other works of mine. Some of these are written in the same manner, suitable for singing [as they stand], since I have indicated in the voice part tremolos, trills, and other new effects not often seen in print, with *passaggi* [diminutions] that are most appropriate for the voice. I have chosen not to demonstrate at this time greater variety in these *passaggi,* since in my opinion there is enough as is for thorough practice in the art, and since I have taken care not to repeat the same sort many times. The *passaggi* herein can serve as stepping-stones to other more difficult ones (which I shall reveal at another time).

I have included some [songs] which are sung now in tenor range, now in bass, with *passaggi* wholly appropriate for both voices; these are for the use of those naturally gifted in covering the combined ranges of these voices. In the bass [sections] of these, one must make tremolos occasionally on some of the quarter-notes and dotted eighths in descending scales in order to give them the greater grace, force, spirit, and, so to speak, bravura and boldness that are required in this range, which is one that calls for considerably less [sheer] expressiveness than does the tenor. As for the measure or tempo to be taken in these airs: the most important consideration on which it depends is a choice made in conformity with the expression of the words. And as for other rhythmic aspects of the vocal part in this or that section [of a song], I shall rely on the singer's judgment, along with [the counsel in] my published essay of 1601 [*recte* 1602].

stampato discorso del 1601. Hò segnato sopra il Basso da sonarsi, e terze, e
e seste maggiori, e minori indifferentemente tanto per B. quadro, quanto per
B. molle, & ogni altra cosa più necessaria, per rendermi più facile à li manco pe
rìti, che hauessero gusto di esercitarsi in esse; riceuetele cortesi lettori con quello affetto, che io ve le porgo, e viuete felici, &c.

ALCVNI AVVERTIMENTI.

TRE cose principalmente si conuengon sapere da chi professa di ben cantar con
affetto solo. Ciò sono lo affetto, la varietà di quello, e la sprezzatura, lo affetto in chi canta altro non è che per la forza di diuerse note, e di vari accenti cò l tem-
peramento del piano, e del forte vna espressione delle parole, e del concetto, che si pren
dono à cantare atta à muouere affetto in chi ascolta. La varietà nell'affetto, è quel trà
passo, che si fa da vno affetto in vn'altro cò medesimi mezzi, secondo che le parole,
e'l concetto guidano il cantante successiuamente. E questa è da osseruarsi minuta-
mente acciocche con la medesima veste (per dir così) vno non togliesse à rappresenta-
re lo sposo, e'l vedouo. La sprezzatura è quella leggiadria la quale si dà al canto
cò l trascorso di più crome, e si microme sopra diuerse corde cò l quale fatto à tempo, to
gliendosi al canto vna certa terminata angustia, e secchezza, si rende piaceuole, li-
cenzioso, e arioso, sì come nel parlar comune la eloquenza, e la fecondia rende age-
uoli, e dolci le cose di cui si fauella. Nella quale eloquenza alle figure, e à i colori
rettorici assimiglierei i passaggi, i trilli, e gli altri simili ornamenti, che sparsamen
te in ogni affetto si possono tal ora introdurre. Conosciutesi queste cose, crederò con
l'osseruazione di questi miei componimenti, che chi hauerà disposizione al cantare,
potrà per auuentura sortir quel fine, che si desidera nel canto specialmente, che è il
dilettare.

TAVOLA.

Aquei sospir ardenti	2	Se voi lagrime à pieno	19	Gia non l'allaccia	38
A ime luce beate	3	Vaga su spin'ascosa	25	Mentre che fra doglie, e pene	39
Se in questo scolorito	5	L'abella man'vistringo	26	Non al Ciel cotanti lumi	40
S'io viuo anima mia	7	Tutto il dì Piango	27	Amor ch'attendi	41
Seridere gioiose	8	In tristo vmor	28	O piante, ò selue	42
Ohime begl'ochi, e quando	10	Lasso che pur	29	Tu ch'ai le penne amore	43
Dite ò del foco mio	11	Più l'altrui fallo	30	Al fonte al prato	44
O dolce fonte del mio pianto		Torna de torna	30	Aura amorosa	45
amaro	13	Io che l'eta solea	33	O che felice giorno	46
Chio non t'ami cor mio	14	Diseguir falso duce	34	Dalla porta d'orrente	47
Hor, che lungi da voi	15	E poi ch'a mortal	35	Con le luci d'vn bel Ciglio	48
Pien d'amoroso affetto	17	Reggami per pieta	36		
Amor l'ali m'in penna	18	Deh chi d'alloro	37		

Il fine della Tauola.

Errori occorsi nello Stampare ac. 20 sino a 25. non vi è numero, ma l'alfabeto sta bene; a carte 25. al 7 verso alla fine
vi è vna croma che non vi va; a carte 33. nell'aria io che l'eta al decimo verso doue è il b. molle secondo vi va
vna minima nel de sol re.

Plate IV. Second page of preface and table of contents of *Nuove musiche* (1614).
(Courtesy, Biblioteca Nazionale Centrale, Florence)

Above the instrumental bass part I have indicated major and minor thirds and sixths (whether or not there is a B-flat [in the signature]) and all other essential [figurations], to make my music easier for non-experts wishing to train themselves in it.

Please accept these [songs], kind readers, in the same spirit with which I offer them; live happily, etc.

SOME OBSERVATIONS

It is advisable for him who professes to sing alone well, with expression, to know three things. These are: affect, variety of affect, and *sprezzatura* ["negligence"].

Affect, in a singer, is simply [this], that by the power of certain notes and varied stresses, together with modifications of the dynamics, an expression of the words and the [poet's] meaning, projected through song, acts to move the affect of him who is listening.

Variety of affect is that transition from one affect to another, by the same means [mentioned above], the singer being guided by the [changes in the] words and meaning from one moment to another. These must be carefully observed so that, so to speak, the bridegroom and the widower are not clothed alike.

Sprezzatura is that charm lent to a song by a few "faulty" eighths or sixteenths on various tones, together with those [similar "faults"] made in the tempo. These relieve the song of a certain restricted narrowness and dryness and make it pleasant, free, and airy, just as in common speech eloquence and variety make pleasant and sweet the matters being spoken of. To the figures [of speech] and rhetorical shadings in such eloquence correspond the *passaggi*, tremolos, and other such ornaments which can occasionally, here and there, be introduced in any [musical] expression.

With knowledge of these things and study of my compositions herein, I believe that he who has a natural bent for singing will perhaps achieve that goal especially desirable in song: to give pleasure.

Plate V. ''Tutto 'l dì piango'' [16a].
(Courtesy, Biblioteca Nazionale Centrale, Florence)

Plate VI. "Non ha 'l ciel cotanti lumi" [21].
(Courtesy, Biblioteca Nazionale Centrale, Florence)

[1] A quei sospir ardenti

to. _____

[2] Alme luci beate

Al- me lu- ci be- a- te Che dol- ce- men- te_ar- de-

te, Se per si lun - ga_e - ta - te A - man- do_e ri - mi-

ran- do Voi fo - ste_il mio gio - i - re, Or per si lun - ga_e -

ta - te A - man- do_e ri - mem- bran- do Sa - re - te_il mio mar - ti -

re; Al - me lu - ci be - a - - -

[3] Se in questo scolorito languido volto

Se in que - sto sco-lo- ri - to Lan - gui-do

vol-to a-mar _____ non puoi _____ bel-lez - - za, A-ma fe - de,

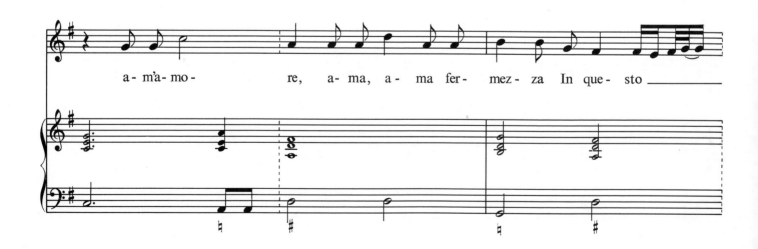

a - m'a-mo - re, a - ma, a - ma fer-mez - za In que - sto _____

cor fe - ri - to. Non è d'amor più deg - no D'u - na fio-ri - ta

guan - cia un cor _____ fe -

de - le? Ma, ma tu pur sem-pre l'a- mo-ro-se ve -

le Spie-ghi al-l'u-sa - to se - gno. Ahi! ahi,

12

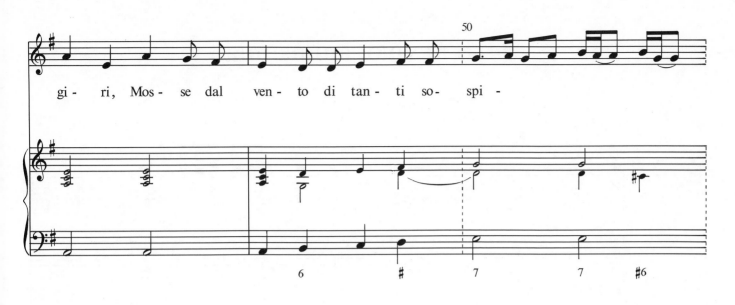

gi - ri, Mos - se dal ven - to di tan - ti so - spi -

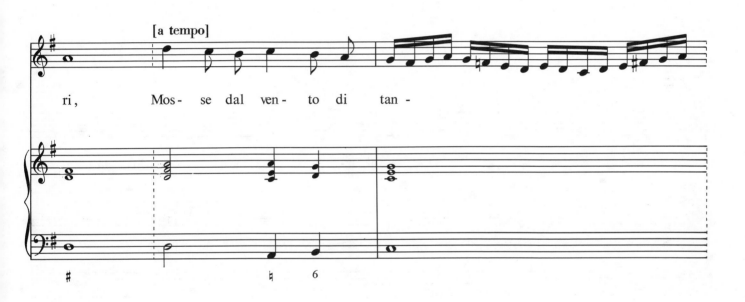

ri, Mos - se dal ven - to di tan -

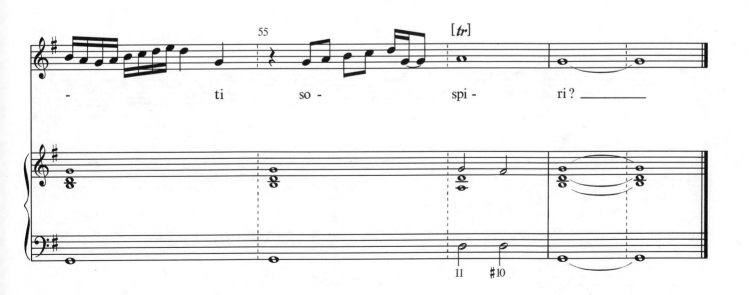

ti so - spi - ri? _____

[4] S'io vivo, anima mia

S'io vi - vo, a - ni - ma _____ mia,

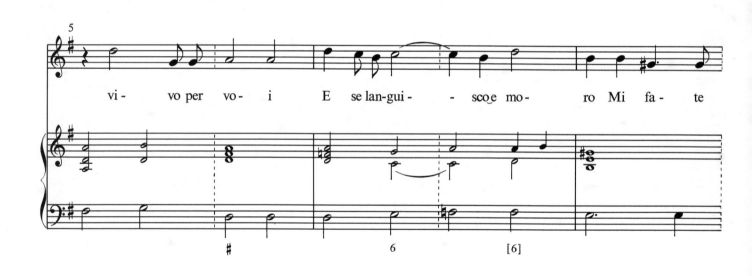

vi - vo per vo - i E se lan-gui - - sco e mo - ro Mi fa - te

voi mo - ri - re, Mi fa - te voi lan - gui -

da è vo- stra col- pa o pur mia sor- te Che sia- te vi- ta e vo- le- t'es- ser

mor- te, e_____ vo- le- t'es- ser mor-

-te; Ma, ma se da voi si bel- l'e si vi- ta- le

Vie- n'ef- fet- to mor- ta- le, Ah!

[5] Se ridete gioiose

Se ri- de- te gio- io- se, Dol- ci lab- bra a- mo-

ro- se, Non sa mo-strar-ne A-mo- re Pre- gio d'a- mor mag-gio-

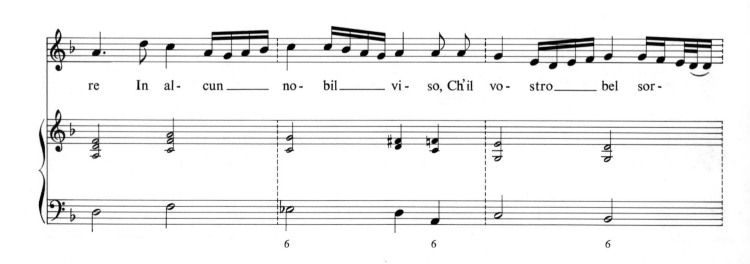

re In al- cun ____ no- bil ____ vi- so, Ch'il vo- stro ____ bel sor-

mo- str'A- mo- re Pre- gio d'a-mor mag- gio- re Nel

vo- stro____ no- bil____ vi- so Col lam-peg- giar d'un____ ri- so,

Se ri- do- no gio- io- si Gli oc-chi vo- stri a-mo- ro-

si, gli oc-chi vo- stri a- mo- ro- si.____

[6] Ohimè, begli occhi

Ohi- mè, ohi- mè, be-gli oc-chi,e quan-do Di mai più ri-ve-

der-vi ha-vrò spe- ran- za Se pria ch'io giun-g'al

tem- po del par-ti- re Già mi_____ sen- to, già mi sen-to mo-

22

ri- re? Spen-de-rò la- gri- man- do Que-sto

po- co di vi- ta che m'a- van- za,____ E'n du- ra lon- ta-

nan- za Pur____ sem- pr'in-van bra- man- do I ____ vo- stri dol-ci

ra- i, Tan- to vi pian-ge- rò, tan- to vi pian-ge- rò quan-

ma -

i.

[7] Dite o del foco mio

[♩= 72]

Di- te o del fo-co mi- o Bel- lis- si-ma ca- gion, lu- ci spie-

ta- te, E___ pur vo- le- te___ ch'i- o, Sen- za spe-rar___ già___

ma- i, In- con- tro al fol- go- rar de' vo- stri ra- i, Scher- mo al- cun di pie-

ta- te, A- man- do e de- si- an- do mi con-

su- mi. Ah! dol- cis- si- mi lu- mi,

Ah! dol- cis- si- mi lu- mi, Non ve- de- te ne- gli oc- chi a-

per -   toil co - re   Che ce - ner fat t'an - cor si

strug - g'e mo -

re? strug - g'e_____ mo -

strug - g'e_____ mo -

re?_____

[8] O' dolce fonte del mio pianto

O', ò dol- ce fon- te del mio pian- to a- ma- ro È pur

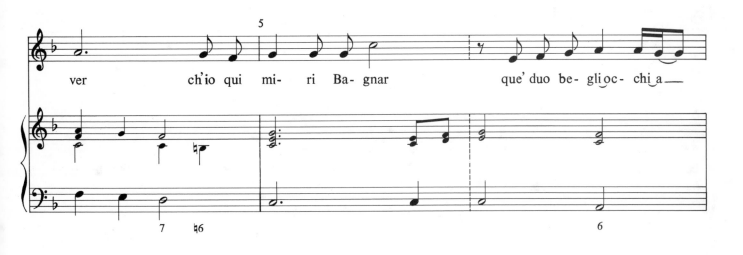

ver ch'io qui mi- ri Ba- gnar que' duo be- gli oc- chi a___

miei so- spi- ri; È ver che ri- spon-dia- t'à __ miei _____ la-

28

mia   ri - vol -   ta in cal -

[6]

- ma   mia   ri - vol -

11   10   7

- ta in cal -   - ma.

11   11   10   7

[9] Ch'io non t'ami cor mio

Ma se tu sei quel cor on - de la vi - ta M'e si dol - c'e gra - di - ta,

Fon - te d'o - gni mio ben, d'o - gni de - si - re, Co - me pos - so las -

sar - ti e non mo - ri - re, Co - me pos - so las - sar - ti e non _____ mo - ri - re?

Fon - te d'o - gni mio ben, d'o - gni de - si - re, Co - me pos - so las - sar - ti e non mo -

32

ri - re, Co - me pos - so las - sar - ti e non _____ mo - ri - re, e

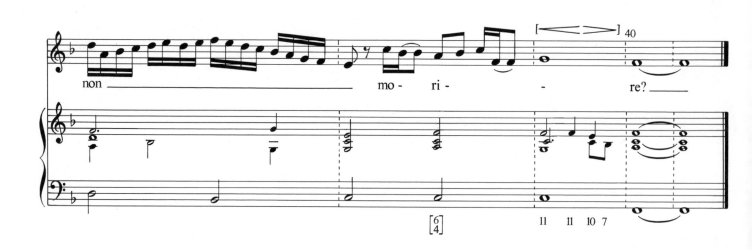

non _____ mo - ri - - re? _____

[10] Hor che lungi da voi

Hor che lun - gi da vo - i Muo - - vo, bei lu - mi,

34

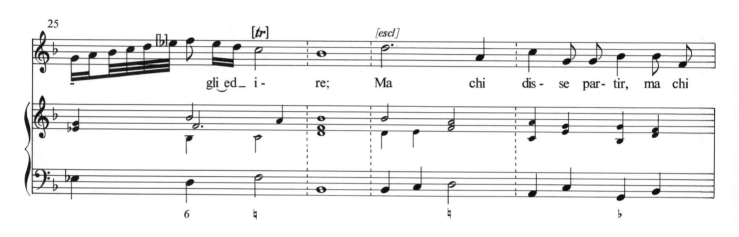

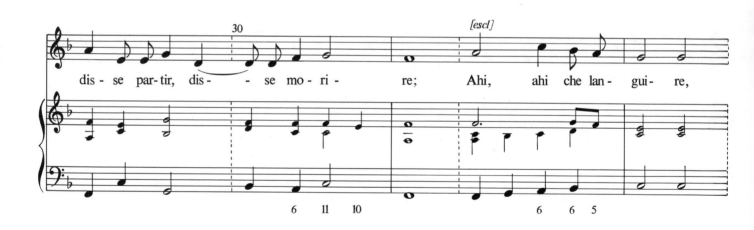

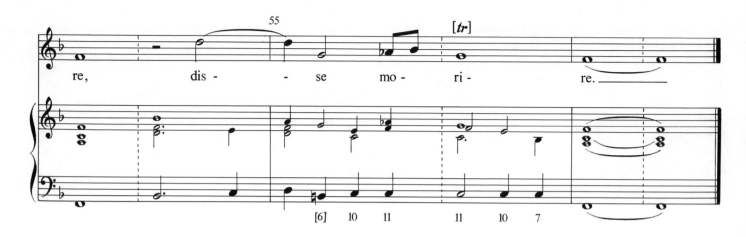

[11] Pien d'amoroso affetto

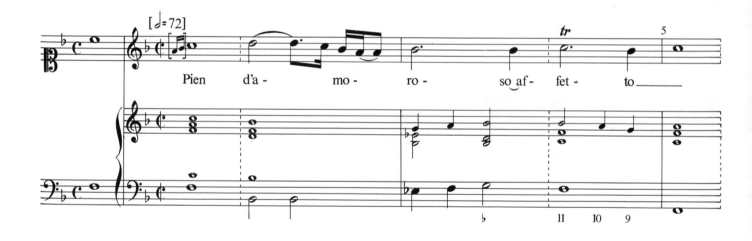

Deh, deh tra-fig-gi-m'il pet - to S'hai ch'io _____ mo - ra di-

let - to. Co - sì dol - ce per lei, co - sì dol - ce per lei lan - guen-

- do ar - de - a. El - la spa - rio di ro - se Il suo bel vol-

to e poi _____ co - sì ri - spo - se:

38

[12] Amor l'ali m'impenna

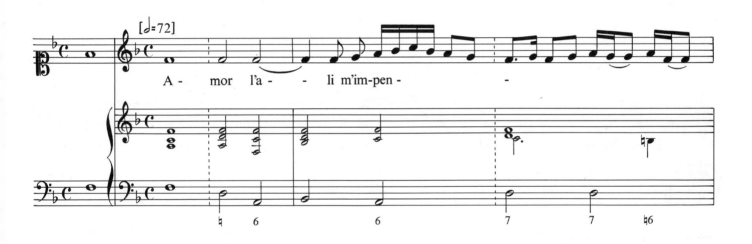

[13] Se voi lagrime a pieno

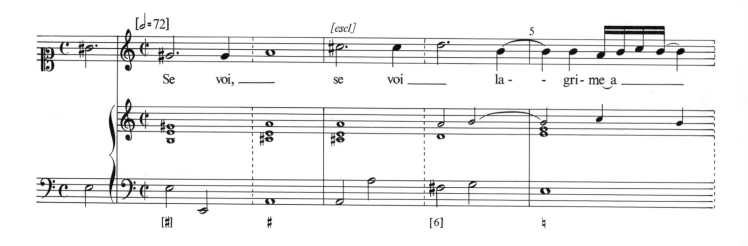

Se voi, ___ se voi ___ la - gri-me a ___

pie - no   Non mo-stra- - te il do -

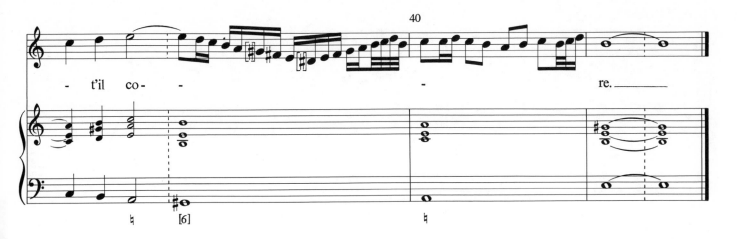

-t'il co- - - re._____

[14] Vaga su spin'ascosa

[♩=72]

Va- ga su spin'a- sco- sa È ro- sa_____ ru- gia-

do- sa, Ch'al- l'al- ba si di- let- ta, Mos- sa da fre- sc'au-

46

[15] La bella man vi stringo

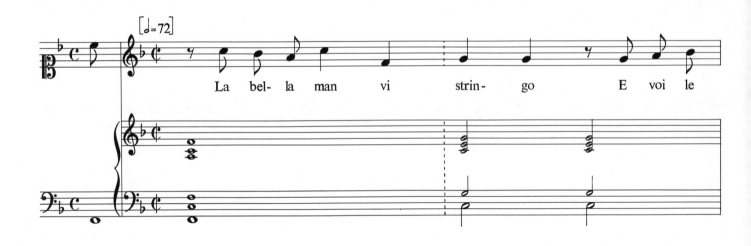

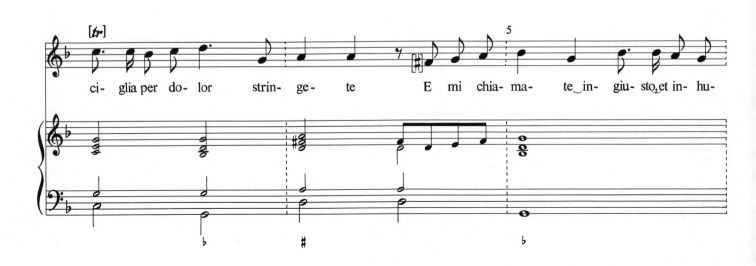

50

lei strin - go il mio _____ co - re, strin - go il mio_____

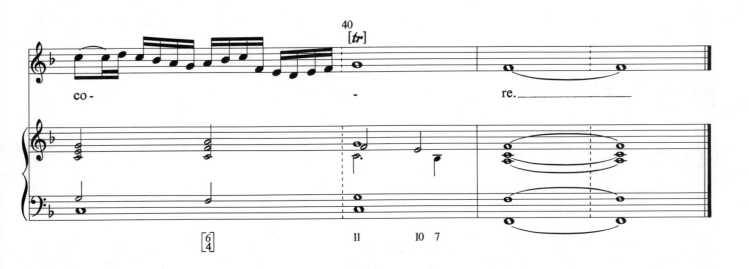

co - re._____

[16a] Tutto 'l dì piango

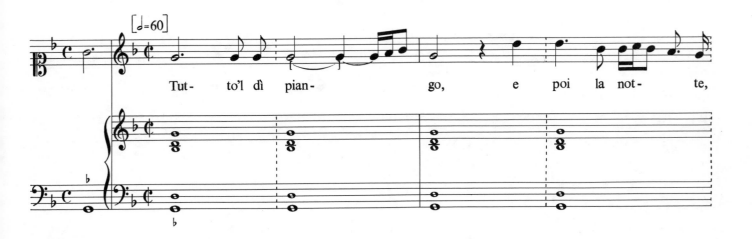

Tut - to'l dì pian - go, e poi la not - te,

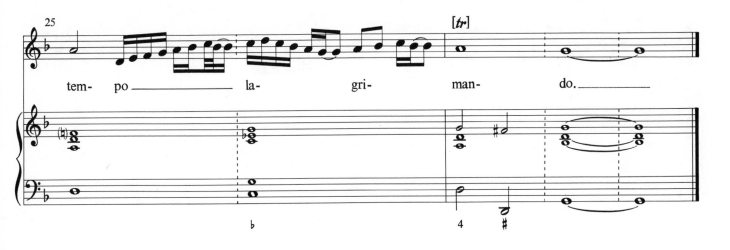

tem- po _____ la- gri- man- do. _____

[16b] In tristo umor

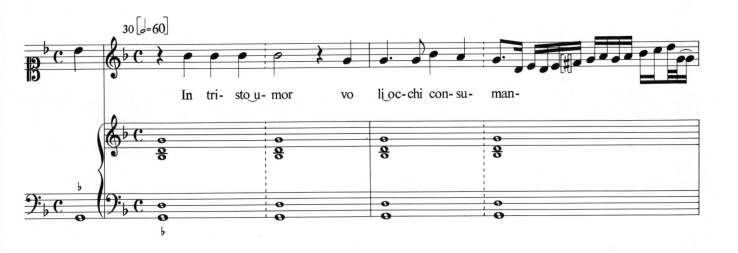

In tri- sto u- mor vo li oc-chi con-su- man-

do, E'l cor in do- glia; e son _____

fra _____ li a- ni- ma-

li   L'ul-   ti- mo,   sì   che li_a- mo- ro- si   stra-

-    -   li   Mi

ten- gon ad   o- gni_or   di   pa-   ce in ban-

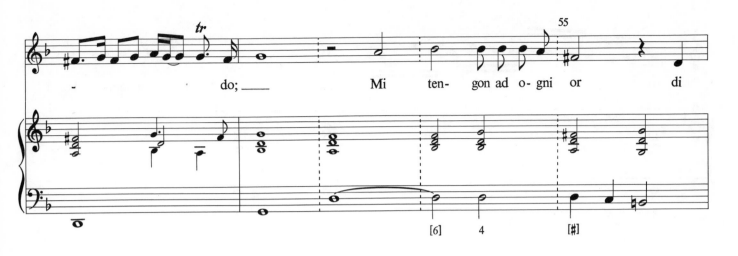

do; _____ Mi ten- gon ad o- gni or di

pa- ce in ___ ban- do. _____

[16c] Lasso, che pur

Las- so, che pur da l'u- no a _____ l'al- tro

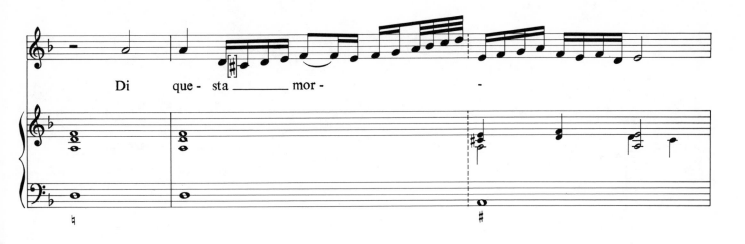

Di que - sta _____ mor -

te che si chia-

[6]

- ma vi - ta. _____

[16d] Più l'altrui fallo

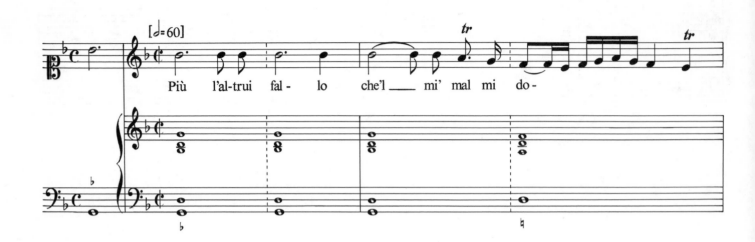

Più l'al-trui fal - lo che'l _____ mi' mal mi do-

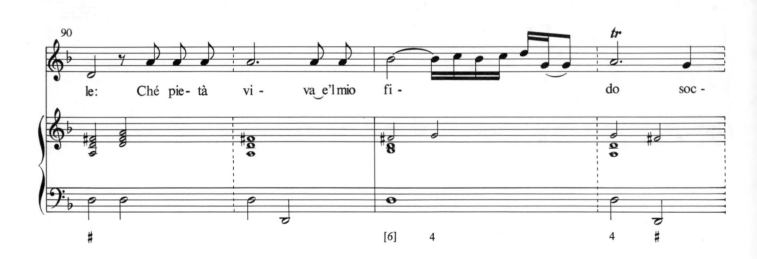

le: Ché pie- tà vi- va e'l mio fi - do soc-

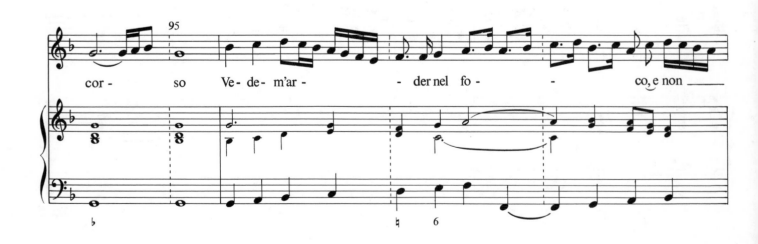

cor- so Ve- de- m'ar - der nel fo - co, e non _____

m'a- i - ta; Ve- de-

m'ar - der nel fo- co,e non _____ m'a i- ta. _____

[17] Torna, deh torna [*Romanesca*]

Tor - na, deh tor - na _____ par- go- let- to mi-

60

mo - - - re? Cor - ri - mi in brac - cio o-mai,

spar - gi___ d'o- bli - - o___

Que - sto,___ che'l cor mi___ strug - ge,a-

spro___ do - lo - re; Que - sto,___ che'l___ cor___ mi

63

64

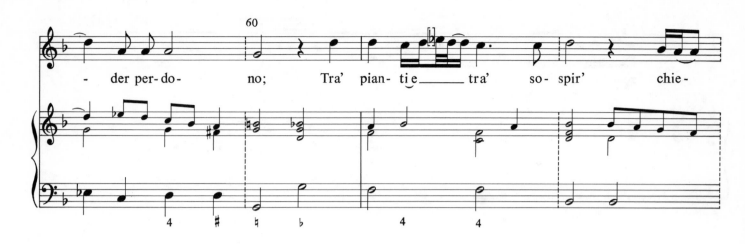

der per-do- no; Tra' pian-ti e_____ tra' so- spir' chie-

der per - do - no._____

[18a] Io, che l'età solea viver nel fango

Io, che l'e- tà_____ so - lea vi - ver nel fan -

[18b] Di seguir falso duce

Di se-guir fal-so du-ce mi ri-man - go; A te mi

do - no; ad o-gni al-tro mi to-glio. Né rot-ta na - ve mai par-tí da

68

[18c] E poi ch'a mortal rischio

E poi ch'a mor-tal ri-schio è gi-ta in- va -

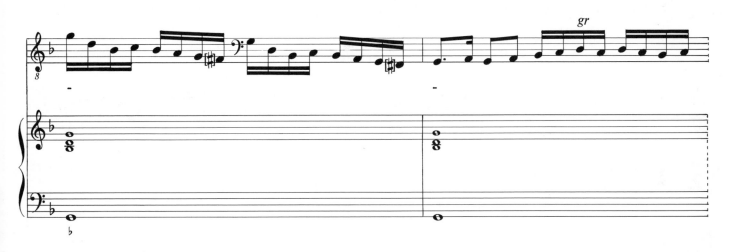

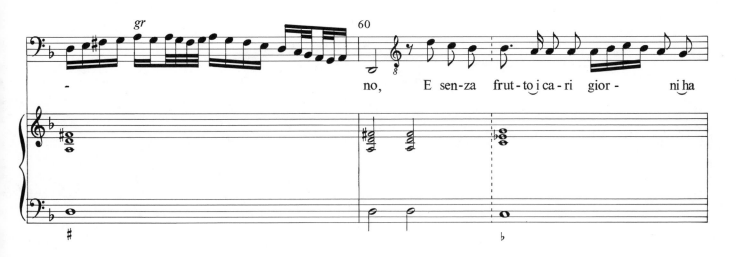

no, E sen-za frut-to i ca-ri gior - ni ha

spe - si Que-sta mia vi - ta, in por - to o - mai ___ l'ac - col -

[6]

4

go; Que-sta mia vi - ta, in ___ por - to o - mai ___

___ l'ac - col -

4

go. ___

[18d] Reggami per pietà

Reg - ga-mi per pie - tà   tua san - ta ma -

- no,   Pa -   dre del ciel,   pa - dre del   ciel,   che

[19a] Deh chi d'alloro

Deh chi d'al - lo - ro Mi fa ghir-lan -

- d'al cri -

74

ne,   Pur mi go - d'io vit - to - ri - o - so al fi - ne   Il

mio _____ te - so - _____ ro,   La

mia __ ne - mi - c'al - te - _____ ra   È

pur _____ mia _____ pri - gio - nie - ra;   La

[19b] Già non l'allaccia

Già non l'al- lac- cia D'a-

spra __ ca- te- n'il __ fer - ro,

Cor-te-se vin-ci-tor tra le mie brac-cia La guar-

[20] Mentre che fra doglie e pene

Men- tre che fra do- glie e pe- ne _____ Nu- tr'il

cor _____ spir- to di spe- me _____ Tras- s'i dì _____ lie - ti e con-

ten- ti _____ Ne gli af- fan- ni e ne i tor- men- ti _____ Or di

Mentre che dolce mia vita
Non ti spiacque darmi aita
Sai ben tu che strali, e foco,
Mi fur sempre festa, e gioco;
Hor non posso, il vo pur dire,
Star nel foco e non morire.

Mentre che cruda e severa
Pur ti mostri, e vuoi ch'io pera,
Mi morrò, nè tu potrai
Darmi aita oimè, che fai?
Vorrai tu ch'a si gran torto,
Chi t'adora resti morto?

Mentre che tra pace e guerra
Viveran gli amanti in terra,
Sia pur fera, e sia crudele
Ti sarò servo fedele
Che se ben tal hor mi doglio
Non per questo a te mi toglio.

[21] Non ha 'l ciel cotanti lumi

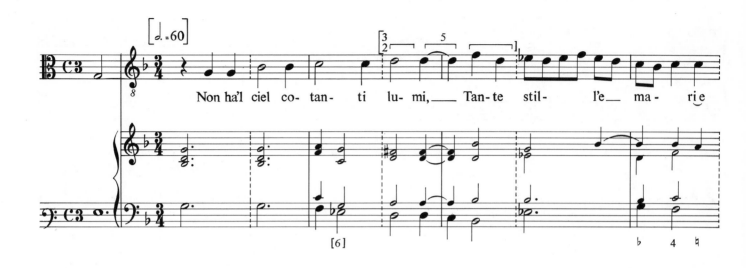

Non ha'l ciel co- tan- ti lu- mi,___ Tan-te stil- l'e___ ma- rie

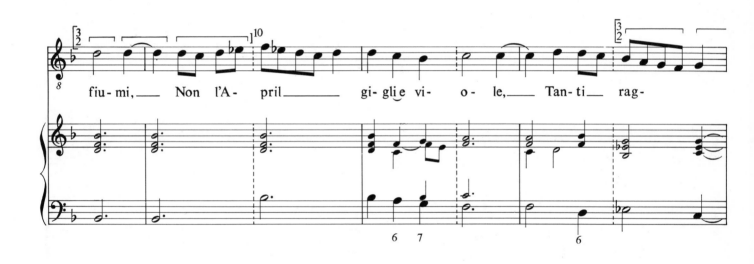

fiu-mi,___ Non l'A- pril___ gi- gli e vi- o- le,___ Tan-ti rag-

gi non ha il So- le,___ Quant'ha do- glie e pe- n'o- gni o- ra___ Cor gen-

Penar lungo e gioir corto,
Morir vivo e viver morto,
Spem' incerta e van desire,
Mercè poca a gran languire,
Falsi risi e veri pianti
È la vita degli amanti.

Neve al sol e nebbia al vento,
E d'Amor gioia e contento,
Degli affanni e delle pene
Ahi che 'l fin già mai non viene,
Giel di morte estingue ardore
Ch'in un'alma accende amore.

Ben soll'io che 'l morir solo
Può dar fine al mio gran duolo,
Nè di voi già mi dogl'io
Del mio stato acerbo e rio;
Sol' Amor tiranno accuso,
Occhi belli, e voi ne scuso.

[22] Amor ch'attendi

Amor ch'at-ten-di, A-mor che fa- i? Su, che non__ pren-di

Gli stra-li o-ma- i; A- mor ven-det - ta, A- mor sa-et - ta

Quel cor ch'al-te- ro Sde-gna'l tuo im-pe- ro; Quel cor ch'al- te- ro

O' pompa, ò gloria,	Quel cor superbo
O' spoglie altere,	Langue e sospira,
Nobil vittoria	Quel viso acerbo
S'Amor la fere;	Pietate spira.
Amor ardisci,	Fatti duoi fiumi
Amor ferisci,	Quei crudi lumi,
Amor et odi	Pur versan fore
Qual havrà i lodi?	Pianto d'amore.
Amor possente	Se cruda e ria
Amor cortese	Negò mercede,
Dirà la gente	Humile e pia
Pur arse e prese	Mercede hor chiede.
Quella crudele,	O' face, ò strale,
Che, di querele	Alta immortale,
Vaga, e di pianti,	Che fia che scampi
Schernia gli amanti.	Si 'l giaccio avvampi.

Dall'alto cielo
Fulmina Giove,
L'Arcier di Delo
Saette piove,
Ma lo stral d'oro
S'orni d'alloro
Che di possanza
Ogni altro avanza.

[23] O piante, o selve ombrose

O pian-te o sel- ve om-bro- se, O val- li o ri- ve er- bo- se, Fio- ri- ti

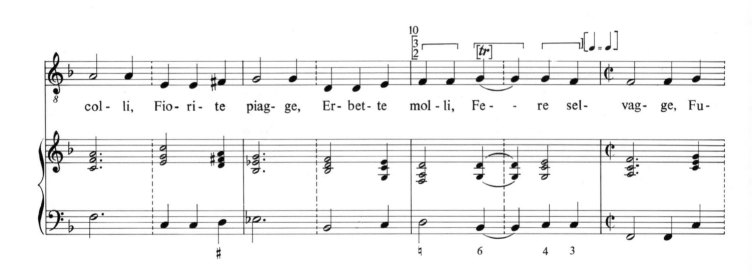

col- li, Fio- ri- te piag- ge, Er- bet- te mol- li, Fe - - re sel- vag- ge, Fu-

ga- ce e fre- sco ri - o, Pie- tà del mo- rir mi - o, Pie- tà del

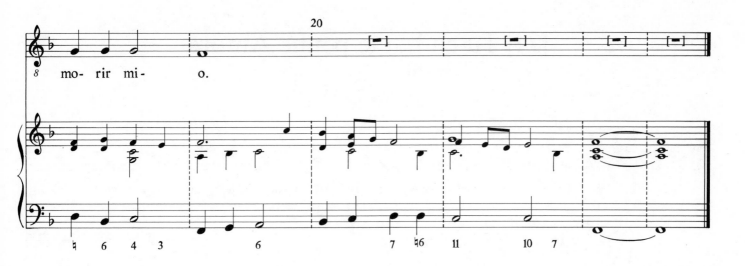

mo- rir mi - o.

Soffrir tanti martiri,
Nutrir tanti sospiri,
Versare stille
Da gli occhi fore
A mille a mille
Più non può 'l core:
Può solo e vuol morire
Pe 'l suo dolor finire.

Già vissi nel tormento
E nel dolor contento,
E i sospir miei
E'l pianto amaro
Sparso per lei
Già mi fu caro;
Hor m'è si aspro e forte
Ch'io bramo la mia morte.

Per donna ch'è si bella,
Che ne rassembra stella,
Lieto penai
Quando mercede
Trovar pensai
A la mia fede;
Ma hor ch'io non lo spero
Accuso il mio pensiero.

Haver qualche pietade
Credei tanta beltade,
Che non inferno,
Ma paradiso,
S'io ben discerne,
Sembra quel viso,
E'l cor apersi stolto,
A i colpi del bel volto.

Crescendo a poco a poco
Venuto è poi quel foco
Che 'l dolce sguardo
M'avventò al seno,
Si ch'io tutt' ardo
Venendo meno,
Nè lasso più speranza
Di refrigerio avanza.

[24] Tu ch'hai le penne Amore

Tu ch'hai le pen- ne A- mo- re E sai spie- gar- le a vo- lo,

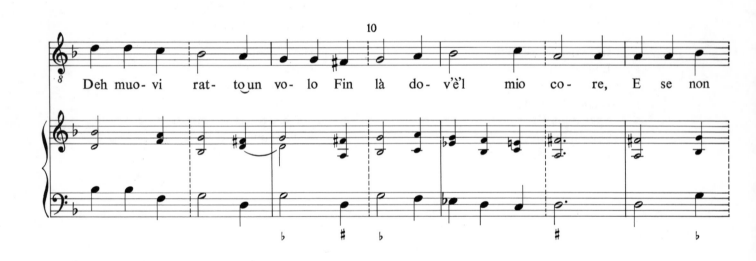

Deh muo- vi rat- to un vo- lo Fin là do- v'è'l mio co- re, E se non

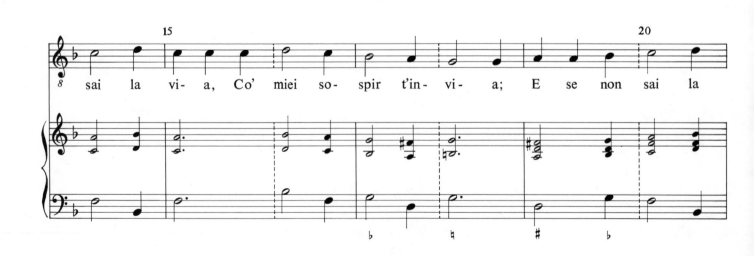

sai la vi- a, Co' miei so- spir t'in- vi- a; E se non sai la

Va pur ch'il troverrai
Tra 'l velo e 'l bianco seno,
O tra 'l dolce sereno
De' luminosi rai,
O tra bei nodi d'oro
Del mio dolce tesoro.

Vanne lusinga, e prega
Perchè dal bel soggiorno
Faccia il mio cor ritorno,
E se'l venir pur niega,
Rivolto al nostro sole,
Digli cotai parole:

Quel tuo fedele amante,
Tra lieta amica gente,
Vive mesto e dolente,
E col tristo sembiante
D'ogni allegrezza spento
Turba l'altrui contento.

Di che fra 'l canto e 'l riso
Spargo sospir di foco,
Che fra 'l diletto e'l gioco
Non mai sereno il viso,
Che d'alma e di cor privo
Stommi fra morto e vivo.

S'entro alle tepide onde
D'Arno, fra lauri e faggi
Fuggon gli estivi raggi,
Io, su l'ombrose sponde
O 'n su l'ardente arena,
Resto carco di pena.

Se dal sassoso fondo
Il crin stillante e molle
Orcheno, il capo e i stolle
Di preda il sen fecondo
Ove ognun un correr' miro
A pena un guardo io giro.

Mentre per piagge e colli
Seguon fugaci fiere
Le cacciatrici fiere;
Lass'io con gli occhi molli
Hor del cesto, hor del resco
L'onda piangendo accresco.

Non degli augei volanti
Miro le prede e i voli
Sol perchè mi consoli
Versar sospiri e pianti—
Ma dì ch'io non vorrei
Far noti i dolor' miei.

Amor cortese impetra
Ch'a me torni il cor mio
O ch'ella il mandi, ond'io
Più non sembri huom di pietra
Nè più con tristo aspetto
Turbi l'altrui diletto.

Ma se per mia ventura
Del suo tornar dubbiosa
Mandarlo a me non osa,
Amor prometti e giura,
Che suo fu sempre, e sia
Il core a l'alma mia.

[25] Al fonte, al prato

Al fon-te,al pra - to, Al bo-sco,a l'om- bra, Al fre - sco fia - to

Ch'il cal - do sgom-bra, Pa-stor cor - re - te; Cia-scun ch'a se - te, Cia - scun ch'e

stan - co Ri- po - s'il fian - co; Cia-scun ch'è stan - co Ri- po - s'il

fian- co.

Fugga la noia,
Fugga il dolore,
Sol riso e gioia,
Sol caro amore.
Nosco soggiorni
Ne' lieti giorni.
Nè s'odan mai
Querele o lai.

Ma dolce canto
Di vaghi uccelli
Pe 'l verde manto
Degli arbuscelli
Risuoni sempre
Con nuovi tempre,
Mentre ch'a l'onde
Ecco risponde.

E mentre alletta
Quanto più puote
La giovinetta
Con rozze note
Il sonno dolce,
Ch'il caldo molce,
E noi pian piano
Con lei cantiano.

[26] Aur'amorosa

Au - r'a - mo - ro - sa   Che dol - ce - men - te____

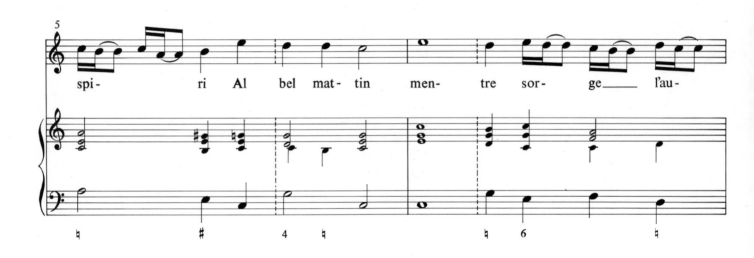

spi - ____ ri   Al bel mat - tin men - tre sor - ge____ l'au -

ro - ____ ra,   Deh spi - r'o - gnio - ra,   Deh, _____ [eh] _____ spi - r'o -

gni o - ra.

Portane teco
Dal celeste sereno
Di perle un vago e rugiadoso nembo
A i fiori in grembo.

E teco insieme
Veng' Amor, Gioco e Riso;
L' Hore, le Gratie e le dotte sorelle
Venghino anch'elle.

Sgombrine omai
L'ardir ch'incenerisce
Il monte e 'l piano, e fa ch'al tuo valore
Respiri il core.

Aprirne un giorno
Viè più che mai tranquillo
Si ch'ogni spirto tua mercè ravvive
In queste rive.

[27] O che felice giorno

O che fe - li - ce___ gior-no, O che___ lie - to___ ri -

tor - no, Rav - vi - va il cor_____ già spen - to.

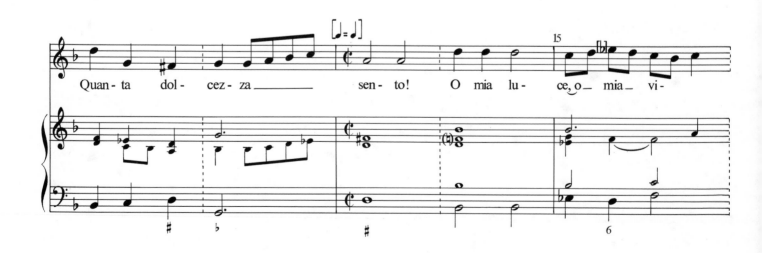

Quan - ta dol - cez - za_____ sen - to! O mia lu - ce, o mia vi -

Ecco 'l mio ben ritorna,
E queste rive adorna;
Eccone lieto il giro
Del bel guardo ch'io miro.
Occhi belli, occhi cari,
Occhi del sol più chiari.

Hor ben prov'io nel petto
Non dolor' ma diletto;
Torna la chiara e bella
Mia rilucente stella,
Torna il Sol, torna l'aura,
Torna chi mi restaura.

Dolce hor mia vita rende
Quel Dio ch'i cori accende;
Amor che l'havea tolto
Hor mi rende il bel volto.
Il mio cor, il mio bene,
Il mio conforto e speme.

[28] Dalla porta d'oriente

Dal- la por - ta d'o - ri - en - te Lam-peg - gian-do in ciel u-

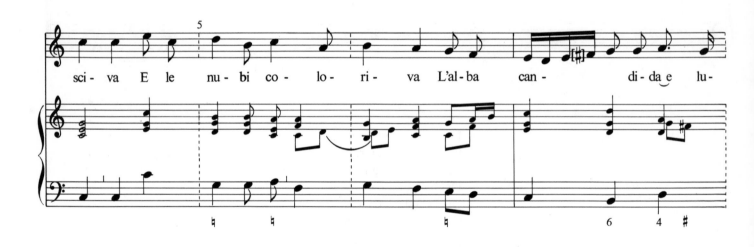

sci - va E le nu - bi co - lo - ri - va L'al - ba can - di - da_e lu -

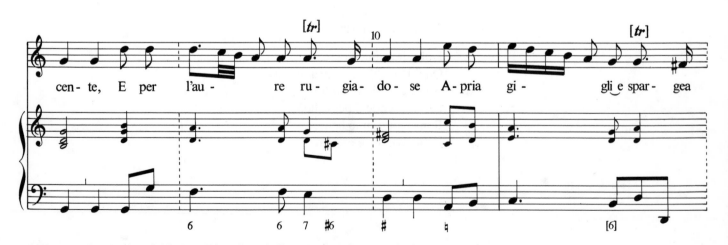

cen - te, E per l'au - re ru - gia - do - se A - pria gi - gli_e spar - gea

* These marks, (l), along with the solid barlines, indicate barline placement in the source.

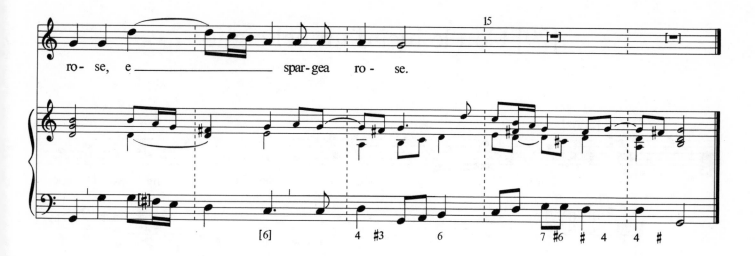

ro- se, e ——————— spar-gea ro- se.

Quand'al nostr'almo terreno
Distendendo i dolci lampi
Vide aprir su i nostri campi
D'altra luce altro sereno;
E portando altr'alba il giorno
Dileguar la notte intorno.

Ch'a sgombrar l'oscuro velo
Più soave e vezzosetta,
Una vaga giovinetta
Accendea le rose in cielo,
E di fiamme porporine
Feria l'aure matutine.

Era il crine a l'aria sparso
Onde l'oro apria suo riso,
E la neve del bel viso
Dolce porpora havea sparso,
E su'l collo alabastrino
Biancheggiava il gelsomino.

Da le labbra innamorate,
Muov' Amor con novi strali,
E di perle orientali
Se ne gian l'alme fregiate,
Et ardeva i cor meschini
Dolce foco di rubini.

Di due splendide facelle
Tanta fiamma discendea,
Che la terra intorno ardea
Et ardeva in ciel le stelle;
E se'l sole usciva fuora,
Havrebb'arso il sole ancora.

Dov'il piè con vago giro,
Dove l'occhio amor partia,
Ogni passo un fiore apria,
Ogni sguardo un bel zaffiro;
E s'udia più dolc'e lento
Mormorar con l'acqua il vento.

L'alba in ciel s'adira e vede
Che le toglie il suo splendore
Questa nova alba d'amore,
E già volge in dietro il piede,
E stillar d'amaro pianto
Già comincia il roseo manto.

[29] Con le luci d'un bel ciglio

* See note on No. [28].

ta - te; Con bei cri - ni Mi com - bat - te em - pia bel -

ta - te.

Ad ogni hor mi dona assalto,
O che in alto
Sproni Febo i suoi destrieri
O ch'in mar' sue fiamme chiuda
E la cruda
Chiama in campo i miei pensieri.

Ah da lei fuggir lontano
Lasso in vano.
Il sudor per me s'impiega
Perch'Amor par che l'a'mpiumi
Si sui fiumi,
E su'l mar' le insegna spiega.

Hor chi porge alcun' ahita
A mia vita?
Se fuggir non ho possanza,
Ch'io contrasti alcun non dica
Tal nemica
Soverchiar non è possanza.